A HOLISTIC GUIDE TO BEING YOUR BEST

Discovering Your Excellence Within

WORKBOOK

Dr. Nick T. Pappas

Copyright © 2022, 2017, Nicholas T. Pappas
All rights reserved.

No part of this book may be reproduced, transmitted, or distributed in any form or by any known or futuristic means, electronic or mechanical, including photocopying, scanning, recording, and/or by any information retrieval system, without the expressed written permission of the author and publisher.

ISBN-13: 978-1-7363651-1-3
Library of Congress Control Number: 2022903764

Millpond Books is a division of Personal and Athletic Solutions, LLC.
14621 New Millpond Road
Big Rapids, MI 49307

Book design and production by Smythtype Design

Disclaimer: This workbook contains new ideas, tools, exercises, and various strategies. The author's intent is to offer information that can assist your quest to enrich your spiritual, mental, emotional, energetic, physical, and relational well-being. The author does not provide medical advice or prescribe the use of any methods as a form of treatment for any kind of medical problems. Always consult with your primary healthcare provider and/or physician when considering the use of new information. For those who decide to make use of any information or strategies found within this workbook, the author Nick Pappas and the publisher make no claims or promises regarding the success that you may or may not experience; therefore, they assume no responsibility and/or liability whatsoever for the use of information from this book. Each reader assumes all responsibility for the use of information from this book.

DEDICATION

This book is dedicated to achievers from all walks of life who strive for excellence in who they are and in all they do.

Table of Contents

INTRODUCTION: Taking the Path to Personal Excellence 6
CHAPTER 1 Exercises for Examining How Badly You "Want" Something 8
CHAPTER 2 Exercises for Examining Pressures, Adversity, and Gifts From Achievement 24
CHAPTER 3 Exercises for Keeping a Balanced Self 36
CHAPTER 4 Exercises for Plugging Your Energy Leaks 45
CHAPTER 5 Exercises for Busting Stress Before It Busts You 60
CHAPTER 6 Exercises for Examining Energy Highs and Lows 81
CHAPTER 7 Exercises for Overcoming the Adversary of Negative Thinking 87
CHAPTER 8 Exercises for Unleashing the Power of Sustained Thought 98
CHAPTER 9 Exercises for Tapping Into the Power of the Present Moment 104
CHAPTER 10 Exercises for Creating Through Visualization 109
CHAPTER 11 Exercises for Avoiding Toxic Communication 125
CHAPTER 12 Exercises for Developing Deeper Bonds and Friendships 137
CHAPTER 13 Exercises for Strengthening Intimate Relationships 148
CHAPTER 14 Exercises for Taking Control of Your Emotional Self 162
CHAPTER 15 Exercises for Finding Passion and Purpose in Your Life's Work 172
CHAPTER 16 Exercises for Activating and Allowing Greater Flow 196
CHAPTER 17 Exercises for Promoting Deeper Connection 210
CHAPTER 18 Exercises for Building Spiritual Connection and Muscle 217
CHAPTER 19 Exercises for Unleashing Power Through Meditation 229
CHAPTER 20 Exercises for Improving as a Role Model, Teacher, and Mentor 241

Further Reading 248
Acknowledgements 252
About the Author 253
Final Blessing 255

INTRODUCTION
Taking the Path to Personal Excellence

Many of today's challenges, imbalances, and illnesses result from man's failure to learn and then do with consistency the work that can lead to greater levels of personal excellence, self-mastery, and eventual wholeness.

People today are faced with an explosion of unique and harmful adversities that are challenging our health, well-being, and wholeness as never before. For instance, our already compromised environment faces constant threats from an array of damaging industries, global warming, devastating toxins, and pollution that harm and alter the landscape of the planet on a daily basis. Then, there are the ever-present dangers involving domestic, political, and foreign aggression, newly emerging bacterial and viral illnesses creating pandemics, along with threats including biological, psychological, societal, and technological sabotage and injuries of all kinds. In addition, the instability lurking in the economy and numerous institutions, including our family, educational, and labor-related environments, means that we have a recipe for experiencing potentially enormous levels of stress, which can lead to anxiety, depression, depletion, and despair. Certainly, the world can appear to be a very gloomy, toxic, and exhausting place to live; plus, this can seem especially true whenever humanity fails to realize, learn, and then remember to use with consistency the many tools and strategies that exist within, which can help to negate and reverse the harmful effects that people would ordinarily be vulnerable to.

Yes, you read correctly that there is a holistic (or whole person) approach that can help lead you to experiencing greater levels of personal excellence, self-mastery, and eventual wholeness. The good news is that the game plan and "how to" guide for this remarkable practice resides within the workbook exercises that you are holding in combination with the accompanying book entitled, *Discovering Your Excellence Within: A Holistic Guide to Being Your Best*. This means that your path to a new and different way of thinking, speaking, acting, being, and living can start the moment you begin doing the exercises you learn and then regularly applying the material each day. Just as a teacher cannot study for a student and a coach cannot compete for an athlete, it is up to each individual achiever to learn and then use with consistency the new ideas, tactics, and techniques that can potentially change the course of their life. Indeed, such work always remains in the hands of an achiever in the making, and this means that authentic knowing of all new information always involves some aspect of doing in combination with dedicated use of the tools and strategies that become part of this learning. In short, to know and not do, is to not really know, because while knowing about something is always better than not knowing, the information will not help you at all without committed use and application of the material. Reminding yourself often that knowing always involves doing something is perhaps one of the best gifts that you can give to your future self.

When completing this workbook, keep an open mind toward any new information and its use until the material can be carefully pondered. Some of the material may be foreign so having an open mind to any new ideas and techniques is essential. I always suggest doing your own experiments to see firsthand which new tools and strategies work best for you. By doing this, you will find that some information will be used more often, while other ideas may be saved for a later time or set aside completely. Wise individuals do not reject new ideas and techniques without carefully testing the information for themselves. Most importantly, by testing the different material thoroughly, each individual will discover what is most useful when striving for personal goals and greater levels of excellence.

I have experienced and observed that learning and then using these ideas will promote more excellence, change lives for the better, and raise consciousness and performance for those choosing to apply this information on a frequent basis. The information has been tested, retested, and used by various visionaries as well as by myself and many other achievers on their path to greater self-mastery, so there is no question that it can produce positive results. How soon the process will start to work always relates to each person's motivation and commitment to persistent use and practice. Plus, with few works available that promote excellence in both the "doing" and "being" aspects of the self from a true holistic perspective, I am confident that this information will be extraordinarily helpful—as it promotes remarkable ways for achieving personal excellence, greater well-being, and eventual wholeness.

Therefore, ask yourself these questions: If you could reach closer to your full potential as an individual and in everything you did, but had to use unfamiliar ideas and techniques to get you there, would you try them? Would you give them a chance? This is what it all comes down to—keeping an open mind to using new concepts, new information. You have nothing to lose and everything to gain from using this material. I give my best regards to everyone learning, using, and applying this information knowing that this workbook and guide will help to make the road to greater levels of excellence, self-mastery, and wholeness a much shorter and enjoyable trip.

Nick T. Pappas
Big Rapids, Michigan

CHAPTER 1
Future Vision Exercises

Envisioning Your Life Path and All That You Would Like to Do

The following exercises, like many others in this workbook, may require more space and paper than this manual has provided. Keeping a tablet or journal specifically for these exercises will enable you to organize, record, and reflect upon your thoughts and work at a later time.

1a). Think about where you want to be in four years and what, specifically, you want to be doing. Discuss the future you imagine below and detail as many areas as possible (i.e., type of schooling, career, sports, activities, hobbies, relationship(s), number of children, geographic location, personal values, and ideals while describing the type of person you would like to be).

b). Next, discuss your general game plan for achieving some of your goals, which will provide a brief map with various ways to help you reach your destination. The exercises that follow will also assist you in determining the processes and plan for helping you to achieve your desires.

2a). Now think about where you want to be in eight years and what you want your life to be like. Discuss the future you imagine below and detail as many areas as possible (i.e., type of schooling, career, sports, activities, hobbies, relationship(s), number of children, geographic location, personal values, and ideals while describing the type of person you would like to be).

b). Next, discuss your general game plan for achieving your three main goals, which will provide a brief map with different ways to help you reach your destination. The exercises that follow will also assist you in determining the processes and plan for helping you to achieve your desires.

CH 1: My Personal "Want" List – Part A

List two things you really "want" and desire in the next 1-3 months.

Short-Term Want #1

Describe the specific steps you will take to get this.

Short-Term Want #2

Describe the specific steps you will take to get this.

List something you really "want" in the next 3-6 months.

Short-Term Want #3

Describe the specific steps you will take to get this.

CH 1: My Personal "Want" List – Part B

List a medium-term "want" that you really desire in the next 1-2 years.

Medium-Term Want #1

Describe the specific steps you will take to get this.

List a long-term "want" that you really desire in the next 4-6 years.

Long-Term Want #2

Describe the specific steps you will take to get this.

Now, list three specific areas of the Self that you would especially like to improve during this next year. Example: I want to manage my stress better (energetic self). I want to work at being more kind and accepting by ending my tendency to judge and speak negatively (spiritual self).

CH 1: Individual Interest Goal Sheet – Part A

Use the following worksheets to detail your plan for achieving each of your identified goals. Refer to pages 15-16 for an example of how this exercise can be completed.

POINTS TO PONDER	AREA(S) OF FOCUS
Goals should be Observable and Measurable	Physical / Mental-Intellectual
Goals should be Challenging yet Achievable	Emotional / Energetic / Relational
Goals should include a Process and Game Plan	Spiritual / Combination of Areas

Write your goal and specify the area(s) of focus this will include.

Current Level of Motivation (How much do you really want to achieve this goal?)

Lowest   Highest

1   2   3   4   5   6   7   8   9   10

Little Interest   Possibility   I Will Achieve My Goal

Process and Game Plan for Reaching This Goal

Doing behaviors that help to achieve this goal.

Thinking practices that help to achieve this goal.

New ways of speaking that help to achieve this goal.

CH 1: Individual Interest Goal Sheet – Part B

Spiritually-connecting practices that help to achieve this goal.

List the people who will support you in achieving this goal and briefly describe their assistance.

_____-

_____-

_____-

Current Discipline Level (i.e., consistency, intensity, and drive needed for achieving this goal)

Lowest   Highest

1   2   3   4   5   6   7   8   9   10

List some ways to raise your discipline level, determination, and drive for reaching this goal.

List some observable ways that others will know you have achieved this goal.

CH 1: Individual Interest Goal Sheet
(Short Version)

Write your goal and specify the area(s) of focus this will include (i.e., physical, mental, emotional, energetic, relational, spiritual, or a combination)

Current Level of Motivation (How much do you really want to achieve this goal?)

Lowest   Highest

1   2   3   4   5   6   7   8   9   10

Little Interest   Possibility   I Will Make My Goal

Process and Game Plan for Reaching This Goal

New Doing Behaviors that help to achieve this goal.

New Thinking Practices that help to achieve this goal.

New Speaking Practices that help to achieve this goal.

Spiritually Connecting Practices that help to achieve this goal.

List the people who will support you in achieving this goal and briefly describe their assistance.

_____ -

_____ -

_____ -

Current Discipline Level (i.e., consistency, intensity, and drive needed to achieve this goal)

Lowest   Highest

1   2   3   4   5   6   7   8   9   10

List some ways to raise your discipline level, determination, and drive for reaching this goal.

List some observable ways that others will know you have achieved this goal.

CH 1: Specific Focus Goal Sheet
(Example of a Special Activity – Part A)

Use the following worksheets to detail your plan for achieving each of your identified goals.

POINTS TO PONDER	AREA(S) OF FOCUS
Goals should be Observable and Measurable	Physical / Mental-Intellectual
Goals should be Challenging yet Achievable	Emotional / Energetic / Relational
Goals should include a Process and Game Plan	Spiritual / Combination of Areas

Write your goal and specify the area(s) of focus this will include.

I would like to become more skilled when doing woodworking projects to the point that I can perhaps earn extra income doing this in my spare time. All areas of the Self are required.

Current Level of Motivation (How much do you really want to achieve this goal?)

Lowest   Highest

1   2   3   4   5   6   **(7)**   8   9   10

Little Interest   Possibility   I Will Achieve My Goal

Process and Game Plan for Reaching This Goal

Doing behaviors that help to achieve this goal.

- *I will begin reading more books and watching videos on ways to increase my skills.*

- *I will spend more time planning and working on these types of projects.*

- *I will talk to more experienced woodworkers to get tips on new tools and learning the craft.*

Thinking practices that help to achieve this goal.

- *I am a can do person that achieves what I set out to do.*

- *I am becoming better and more skilled every day in every way.*

- *I am attracting everything and everyone I need to be successful.*

New ways of speaking that help to achieve this goal.

- *I am on my way to becoming a skilled craftsman.*

- *I am going to increase my income as I increase my woodworking skills.*

- *I am actively seeking new ways to improve my craft.*

CH 1: Specific Focus Goal Sheet
(Example of a Special Activity – Part B)

Spiritually-connecting practices that help to achieve this goal.

- *With God's help and daily prayer, I will achieve all my goals.*

- *I will take time each day to imagine my woodworking becoming better and better.*

- *My constant affirmation: Thank you God my woodworking is getting better every day in every way.*

List the people who will support you in achieving this goal and briefly describe their assistance.

Parents – I will share my plans and goals and allow their ideas to assist my work.

Specific friend(s) – I will ask for ideas and information from people already doing this work.

Professional Organizations – I will join groups that share information and resources with their members.

Current Discipline Level (i.e., consistency, intensity, and drive needed for achieving this goal)

Lowest   Highest

1   2   3   4   5   6   (7)   8   9   10

List some ways to raise your discipline level, determination, and drive for reaching this goal.

- *Take each day, one day at a time, and make progress by increasing my skills.*

- *Make woodworking a major priority in my life each day.*

- *Let friends know they are welcome to visit me at my shop as I focus on my goals.*

List some observable ways that others will know you have achieved this goal.

- *People will make comments on the skillfulness of my woodworking.*

- *I will see more money in my bank account from the projects I sell.*

- *People will seek me out to complete their special projects.*

CH 1: Specific Focus Goal Sheet
(Sports, Music, Acting, Special Activity – Part A)

Use the following worksheets to detail your plan for achieving each of your identified goals.

POINTS TO PONDER	AREA(S) OF FOCUS
Goals should be Observable and Measurable	Physical / Mental-Intellectual
Goals should be Challenging yet Achievable	Emotional / Energetic / Relational
Goals should include a Process and Game Plan	Spiritual / Combination of Areas

Write your goal and specify the area(s) of focus this will include.

Current Level of Motivation (How much do you really want to achieve this goal?)

Lowest   Highest
1   2   3   4   5   6   7   8   9   10
Little Interest   Possibility   I Will Achieve My Goal

Process and Game Plan for Reaching This Goal

Doing behaviors that help to achieve this goal.

Thinking practices that help to achieve this goal.

New ways of speaking that help to achieve this goal.

CH 1: Specific Focus Goal Sheet
(Sports, Music, Acting, Special Activity – Part B)

Spiritually-connecting practices that help to achieve this goal.

List the people who will support you in achieving this goal and briefly describe their assistance.

_____-

_____-

_____-

Current Discipline Level (i.e., consistency, intensity, and drive needed for achieving this goal)

Lowest   Highest
1   2   3   4   5   6   7   8   9   10

List some ways to raise your discipline level, determination, and drive for reaching this goal.

List some observable ways that others will know you have achieved this goal.

CH 1: Specific Focus Goal Sheet
(Sports, Music, Acting, Special Activity – Short Version)

Write your goal and specify the area(s) of focus this will include (i.e., physical, mental, emotional, energetic, relational, spiritual, or a combination)

Current Level of Motivation (How much do you really want to achieve this goal?)

Lowest   Highest
1   2   3   4   5   6   7   8   9   10
Little Interest   Possibility   I Will Make My Goal

Process and Game Plan for Reaching This Goal

New Doing Behaviors that help to achieve this goal.

New Thinking Practices that help to achieve this goal.

New Speaking Practices that help to achieve this goal.

Spiritually Connecting Practices that help to achieve this goal.

List the people who will support you in achieving this goal and briefly describe their assistance.

_____ -

_____ -

_____ -

Current Discipline Level (consistency, intensity, and drive needed to achieve this goal)

Lowest   Highest
1   2   3   4   5   6   7   8   9   10

List some ways to raise your discipline level and drive for reaching this goal.

List some observable ways that others will know you have achieved this goal.

CH 1: Team/Family/Group Goal Sheet

List a team, family, or group goal you "want" in the next 1-3 months. Team "Want" #1.

List some ways you intend to help accomplish this.

List a team, family, or group goal you "want" in the next 3-6 months. Team "Want" #2.

List some ways you intend to help accomplish this.

List a team, family, or group goal you "want" in the next 6-12 months. Team "Want" #3.

List some ways you intend to help accomplish this.

List three specific areas which you would especially like to see your team, family, or group improve on this year. (Example: Better efficiency and productivity by working together more as a unit than as individuals)

CH 1: Team/Family/Group Goal Sheet – Part A

Use the following worksheets to detail your plan for achieving each of your identified goals.

POINTS TO PONDER	AREA(S) OF FOCUS
Goals should be Observable and Measurable	Physical / Mental-Intellectual
Goals should be Challenging yet Achievable	Emotional / Energetic / Relational
Goals should include a Process and Game Plan	Spiritual / Combination of Areas

Write your goal and specify the area(s) of focus this will include.

Current Level of Motivation (How much do you really want to achieve this goal?)

Lowest   Highest

1   2   3   4   5   6   7   8   9   10

Little Interest   Possibility   I Will Achieve My Goal

Process and Game Plan for Reaching This Goal

Doing behaviors that help to achieve this goal.

Thinking practices that help to achieve this goal.

New ways of speaking that help to achieve this goal.

CH 1: Team/Family/Group Goal Sheet – Part B

Spiritually-connecting practices that help to achieve this goal.

List the people who will support you in achieving this goal and briefly describe their assistance.

_____-

_____-

_____-

Current Discipline Level (i.e., consistency, intensity, and drive needed for achieving this goal)

Lowest   Highest
1   2   3   4   5   6   7   8   9   10

List some ways to raise your discipline level, determination, and drive for reaching this goal.

List some observable ways that others will know you have achieved this goal.

CH 1: Team/Family/Group Goal Sheet (Short Version)

Write your goal and specify the area(s) of focus this will include (i.e., physical, mental, emotional, energetic, relational, spiritual, or a combination)

Current Level of Motivation (How much do you really want to achieve this goal?)

Lowest   Highest

1   2   3   4   5   6   7   8   9   10

Little Interest   Possibility   I Will Make My Goal

Process and Game Plan for Reaching This Goal

New Doing Behaviors that help to achieve this goal.

New Thinking Practices that help to achieve this goal.

New Speaking Practices that help to achieve this goal.

Spiritually Connecting Practices that help to achieve this goal.

List the people who will support you in achieving this goal and briefly describe their assistance.

_____-

_____-

_____-

Current Discipline Level (i.e., consistency, intensity, and drive needed to achieve this goal)

Lowest   Highest

1   2   3   4   5   6   7   8   9   10

List some ways to raise your discipline level, determination, and drive for reaching this goal.

List some observable ways that others will know you have achieved this goal.

CHAPTER 2
Internal Pressure-Busting Worksheet – Part A

Briefly describe the internal pressures you are facing and when and how they started. Internal pressures can include your own expectations, desire for control or perfectionism, a need to succeed at all costs, and the internal thoughts you often tell yourself.

List three things you can **do** differently to address and assist the situation.

List three ways to **think** differently about the situation.

List three ways to **spiritually connect and tune-in** to your Source to assist this experience.

CH 2: Internal Pressure-Busting Worksheet – Part B

List three things to positively **affirm and speak** to lessen the pressure and assist the situation.

List three **additional ways to help cope** with this experience.

List three people who can **help support** you in this situation and briefly describe their assistance.

Now take a moment to reflect upon what was most effective in your problem-solving. How well did you do and feel when addressing this issue? What would you do differently next time?

CH 2: Internal Pressure-Busting Worksheet (Short Version)

Briefly describe the type of **internal pressures** you are facing and when and how they started.

List three things you can **do** differently to address and assist the situation.

List three ways to **think** differently about the situation.

List three ways to **spiritually connect and tune-in** to your Source to assist this experience.

List three things to positively **affirm and speak** to lessen the pressure and assist the situation.

List three **additional ways to help cope** with this experience.

List three people who can **help support** you in this situation and briefly describe their assistance.

Now take a moment to reflect upon what was most effective in your problem-solving. How well did you do and feel when addressing this issue? What would you do differently next time?

CH 2: External Pressure-Busting Worksheet – Part A

Briefly describe the external pressures you are facing and when and how they started. External pressures include others' expectations, desire for control or perfectionism, a need to succeed at all costs, and the silent or verbal messages you often receive from outside sources.

List three things you can **do** differently to address and assist the situation.

List three ways to **think** differently about the situation.

List three ways to **spiritually connect and tune-in** to your Source to assist this experience.

CH 2: External Pressure-Busting Worksheet – Part B

List three things to positively **affirm and speak** to lessen the pressure and assist the situation.

List three **additional ways to help cope** with this experience.

List three people who can **help support** you in this situation and briefly describe their assistance.

Now take a moment to reflect upon what was most effective in your problem-solving. How well did you do and feel when addressing this issue? What would you do differently next time?

CH 2: External Pressure-Busting Worksheet (Short Version)

Briefly describe the type of **external pressures** you are facing and when and how they started.

List three things you can **do** differently to address and assist the situation.

List three ways to **think** differently about the situation.

List three ways to **spiritually connect and tune-in** to your Source to assist this experience.

List three things to positively **affirm and speak** to lessen the pressure and assist the situation.

List three **additional ways to help cope** with this experience.

List three people who can **help support** you in this situation and briefly describe their assistance.

Now take a moment to reflect upon what was most effective in your problem-solving. How well did you do and feel when addressing this issue? What would you do differently next time?

CH 2: Media-Related Pressure-Busting Worksheet – Part A

Briefly describe the media-related pressures you are facing and when and how they started. Media-related pressures include messages from television, advertising, The Internet, movies, magazines, books, and other media-related sources that highlight unreal expectations and stereotypes related to physical characteristics, gender roles, positions, and possessions.

List three things you can **do** differently to address and assist the situation.

List three ways to **think** differently about the situation.

List three ways to **spiritually connect and tune-in** to your Source to assist this experience.

CH 2: Media-Related Pressure-Busting Worksheet – Part B

List three things to positively **affirm and speak** to lessen the pressure and assist the situation.

List three **additional ways to help cope** with this experience.

List three people who can **help support** you in this situation and briefly describe their assistance.

Now take a moment to reflect upon what was most effective in your problem-solving. How well did you do and feel when addressing this issue? What would you do differently next time?

CH 2: Media-Related Pressure-Busting Worksheet (Short Version)

Briefly describe the **media-related pressures** you are facing and when and how they started.

List three things you can **do** differently to address and assist the situation.

List three ways to **think** differently about the situation.

List three ways to **spiritually connect and tune-in** to your Source to assist this experience.

List three things to positively **affirm and speak** to lessen the pressure and assist the situation.

List three **additional ways to help cope** with this experience.

List three people who can **help support** you in this situation and briefly describe their assistance.

Now take a moment to reflect upon what was most effective in your problem-solving. How well did you do and feel when addressing this issue? What would you do differently next time?

CH 2: Team/Group-Related Pressure-Busting Worksheet – Part A

Briefly describe the team/group-related pressures you are facing and when and how they started. Team/group-related pressures include messages from peer groups highlighting an array of expectations, need for control or perfectionism, and stereotypes related to all kinds of issues.

List three things you can **do** differently to address and assist the situation.

List three ways to **think** differently about the situation.

List three ways to **spiritually connect and tune-in** to your Source to assist this experience.

CH 2: Team/Group-Related Pressure-Busting Worksheet – Part B

List three things to positively **affirm and speak** to lessen the pressure and assist the situation.

List three **additional ways to help cope** with this experience.

List three people who can **help support** you in this situation and briefly describe their assistance.

Now take a moment to reflect upon what was most effective in your problem-solving. How well did you do and feel when addressing this issue? What would you do differently next time?

CH 2: Team/Group-Related Pressure-Busting Worksheet
(Short Version)

Briefly describe the **team/group-related pressures** you are facing and when and how they started.

List three things you can **do** differently to address and assist the situation.

List three ways to **think** differently about the situation.

List three ways to **spiritually connect and tune-in** to your Source to assist this experience.

List three things to positively **affirm and speak** to lessen the pressure and assist the situation.

List three **additional ways to help cope** with this experience.

List three people who can **help support** you in this situation and briefly describe their assistance.

Now take a moment to reflect upon what was most effective in your problem-solving. How well did you do and feel when addressing this issue? What would you do differently next time?

CHAPTER 3
Balancing and Improving the Holistic Self
(Short Version – Part A)

Briefly discuss a **Physical Pursuit** along with your reasons for wanting to accomplish this. Be sure to explain how this pursuit will help to balance and improve your complete, holistic self.

Briefly discuss an **Energetic** (stress-reducing, energy producing) **Pursuit** along with your reasons for wanting to accomplish this. Then, explain how this pursuit will help to balance and improve your complete, holistic self.

Briefly discuss a **Mental/Intellectual Pursuit** along with your reasons for wanting to accomplish this. Be sure to explain how this pursuit will help to balance and improve your complete, holistic self.

CH 3: Balancing and Improving the Holistic Self
(Short Version – Part B)

Briefly discuss a **Relational/Interactional Pursuit** along with your reasons for wanting to accomplish this. Be sure to explain how this pursuit will help to balance and improve your complete, holistic self.

Briefly discuss an **Emotionally-Based Pursuit** along with your reasons for wanting to accomplish this. Then, explain how this pursuit will help to balance and improve your complete, holistic self.

Briefly discuss a **Spiritual Pursuit** along with your reasons for wanting to accomplish this. Be sure to explain how this pursuit will help to balance and improve your complete, holistic self.

CH 3: Balancing and Improving the Holistic Self – Physical Pursuits

List and briefly describe your physical pursuit.

List three things to **do** each day to accomplish this mission.

List three ways to **think** positively in order to accomplish this quest.

List three ways to **spiritually connect and tune-in** to your Source to accomplish this task.

List three people who can **help and support** you in this work and briefly describe their assistance.

List three ways that achieving this pursuit will be used **to help others**.

CH 3: Balancing and Improving the Holistic Self – Energetic Pursuits

List and briefly describe your energetic (stress-reducing, energy producing) pursuit.

List three things to **do** each day to accomplish this mission.

List three ways to **think** positively in order to accomplish this quest.

List three ways to **spiritually connect and tune-in** to your Source to accomplish this task.

List three people who can **help and support** you in this work and briefly describe their assistance.

List three ways that achieving this pursuit will be used **to help others**.

CH 3: Balancing and Improving the Holistic Self
Mental/Intellectual Pursuits

List and briefly describe your mental/intellectual pursuit.

List three things to **do** each day to accomplish this mission.

List three ways to **think** positively in order to accomplish this quest.

List three ways to **spiritually connect and tune-in** to your Source to accomplish this task.

List three people who can **help and support** you in this work and briefly describe their assistance.

List three ways that achieving this pursuit will be used **to help others**.

CH 3: Balancing and Improving the Holistic Self
Relational/Interactional Pursuits

List and briefly describe your relational/interactional pursuit.

List three things to **do** each day to accomplish this mission.

List three ways to **think** positively in order to accomplish this quest.

List three ways to **spiritually connect and tune-in** to your Source to accomplish this task.

List three people who can **help and support** you in this work and briefly describe their assistance.

List three ways that achieving this pursuit will be used **to help others**.

CH 3: Balancing and Improving the Holistic Self
Emotionally-Based Pursuits

List and briefly describe your emotionally-based pursuit.

List three things to **do** each day to accomplish this mission.

List three ways to **think** positively in order to accomplish this quest.

List three ways to **spiritually connect and tune-in** to your Source to accomplish this task.

List three people who can **help and support** you in this work and briefly describe their assistance.

List three ways that achieving this pursuit will be used **to help others**.

CH 3: Balancing and Improving the Holistic Self
Spiritual Pursuits

List and briefly describe your spiritual pursuit.

List three things to **do** each day to accomplish this mission.

List three ways to **think** positively in order to accomplish this quest.

List three ways to **spiritually connect and tune-in** to your Source to accomplish this task.

List three people who can **help and support** you in this work and briefly describe their assistance.

List three ways that achieving this pursuit will be used **to help others**.

CH 3: Problem-Solving Worksheet

(Adapted from the ideas of Dawn Miles)

1. Describe the **challenge**:

2. List all the **available options** for solving this problem:

a.   c.   e.

b.   d.   f.

3. Identify the **positive (+) and negative (-) consequences** for the better options:

Option ____: Pros (+) and Cons (-) List	Option ____: Pros (+) and Cons (-) List
(+) (+) (+) (-) (-) (-)	(+) (+) (+) (-) (-) (-)
Option ____: Pros (+) and Cons (-) List	Option ____: Pros (+) and Cons (-) List
(+) (+) (+) (-) (-) (-)	(+) (+) (+) (-) (-) (-)

4. Indicate the **best solution** for overcoming this challenge and discuss your reasoning for this:

CHAPTER 4
Identifying Your Energy Leaks

The following activities will help you to identify your energy leaks so that you can discover better ways to problem-solve and then plug all of the drains that are robbing you of valuable energies.

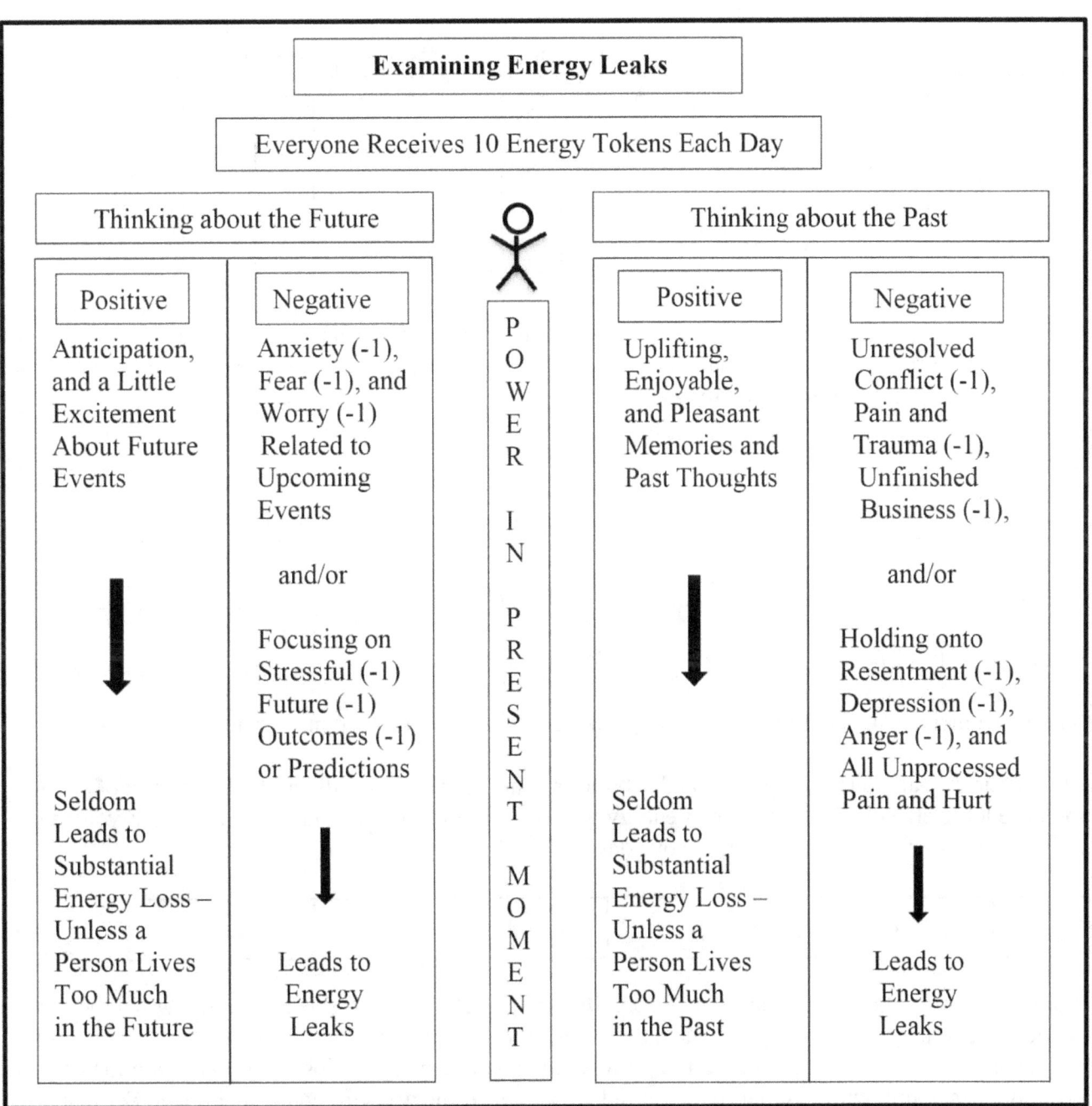

CH 4: Identifying Your Energy Leaks – Part I

(Adapted from the ideas of Dr. Cathy Ely-Grover)

Circle a number in the boxes, which relates to the level of leakage that each category produces. For example, a **level "3" leak** is the largest energy drain which constantly occupies your time and attention. A **level "2"** is a moderate-level leak while a **level "1"** is the lowest type of leak which takes the least amount of your attention, time, and energy.

School	Work	Sport	Special Activity	Family	Friends	Partner	Other Leakage
3	3	3	3	3	3	3	3
2	2	2	2	2	2	2	2
1	1	1	1	1	1	1	1

Now, write the specific nature of the energy leak and its amount (0 - 3) that relates to each category. You do not have to use every category, but noting what specifically causes you to lose energy in each of these areas is an important step to eliminating the leak.

School Leaks - _____ (___)   Family Leaks - _____ (___)

Work Leaks - _____ (___)   Friendship Leaks - _____ (___)

Sport Leaks - _____ (___)   Partnership Leaks - _____ (___)

Special Activity Leaks - _____ (___)   Other Leaks - _____ (___)

(These can include all types of challenges as well as illnesses, injuries, money issues, and losses.)

After adding up all your energy leaks and subtracting this number from 10, circle the amount of energy you have leftover. This is the amount of energy that you have left to fuel your day. Hopefully, you have enough energy leftover to have a productive day.

1	2	3	4	5	6	7	8	9	10

Because it is important to have at least 7 energy tokens per day, the worksheets that follow will help you to find ways to plug your energy leaks and gain more energy to fuel your day and all its activities. This will involve problem-solving to find different ways to lessen your energy losses perhaps with the help of a friend you can talk with in order to discuss a leak and examine ways to reduce its impact. For instance, if your school leak originally took (3) bits of energy and you, perhaps with the help of a friend, figured out some ways to reduce this energy drain, you might write a (2) or a (1) at the end of the following worksheets instead of the (3) which was initially circled in the box. This can only happen **if** you find that **doing** these activities actually lessens your energy leaks and losses.

CH 4: Plugging Your Energy Leaks – School

Briefly describe the situation, how you are losing energy, and your reasoning for rating this leak at its present level after circling a number (minor energy leak) 1   2   3 (major leak).

List three things you will **do** each day to reduce this energy drain.

List three ways that you will **think differently** each day to reduce this energy drain.

List three ways to **spiritually connect and tune-in** to your Source to reduce this energy drain.

List three things to **positively affirm and speak** to lessen and reduce this energy drain.

List three **additional ways to cope** with this situation to reduce this energy drain.

List three **people that will help you** reduce this energy drain and briefly describe their assistance.

Briefly describe how you plan to **"let go" and release** this energy leak from your mind.

Now circle the number which corresponds to the amount of energy you are losing after completing the exercises above for at least a month.

0 = Energy Leak is plugged   (minor energy leak)   1   2   3   (major energy leak)

CH 4: Plugging Your Energy Leaks – Work

Briefly describe the situation, how you are losing energy, and your reasoning for rating this leak at its present level after circling a number (minor energy leak) 1   2   3 (major leak).

List three things you will **do** each day to reduce this energy drain.

List three ways that you will **think differently** each day to reduce this energy drain.

List three ways to **spiritually connect and tune-in** to your Source to reduce this energy drain.

List three things to **positively affirm and speak** to lessen and reduce this energy drain.

List three **additional ways to cope** with this situation to reduce this energy drain.

List three **people that will help you** reduce this energy drain and briefly describe their assistance.

Briefly describe how you plan to **"let go" and release** this energy leak from your mind.

Now circle the number which corresponds to the amount of energy you are losing after completing the exercises above for at least a month.

0 = Energy Leak is plugged   (minor energy leak) 1   2   3 (major energy leak)

CH 4: Plugging Your Energy Leaks – Sports

Briefly describe the situation, how you are losing energy, and your reasoning for rating this leak at its present level after circling a number (minor energy leak) 1 2 3 (major leak).

List three things you will **do** each day to reduce this energy drain.

List three ways that you will **think differently** each day to reduce this energy drain.

List three ways to **spiritually connect and tune-in** to your Source to reduce this energy drain.

List three things to **positively affirm and speak** to lessen and reduce this energy drain.

List three **additional ways to cope** with this situation to reduce this energy drain.

List three **people that will help you** reduce this energy drain and briefly describe their assistance.

Briefly describe how you plan to **"let go" and release** this energy leak from your mind.

Now circle the number which corresponds to the amount of energy you are losing after completing the exercises above for at least a month.

0 = Energy Leak is plugged   (minor energy leak) 1   2   3 (major energy leak)

CH 4: Plugging Your Energy Leaks – Special Activity Leaks

Briefly describe the situation, how you are losing energy, and your reasoning for rating this leak at its present level after circling a number (minor energy leak) 1   2   3 (major leak).

List three things you will **do** each day to reduce this energy drain.

List three ways that you will **think differently** each day to reduce this energy drain.

List three ways to **spiritually connect and tune-in** to your Source to reduce this energy drain.

List three things to **positively affirm and speak** to lessen and reduce this energy drain.

List three **additional ways to cope** with this situation to reduce this energy drain.

List three **people that will help you** reduce this energy drain and briefly describe their assistance.

Briefly describe how you plan to **"let go" and release** this energy leak from your mind.

Now circle the number which corresponds to the amount of energy you are losing after completing the exercises above for at least a month.

0 = Energy Leak is plugged   (minor energy leak) 1   2   3 (major energy leak)

CH 4: Plugging Your Energy Leaks – Family

Briefly describe the situation, how you are losing energy, and your reasoning for rating this leak at its present level after circling a number (minor energy leak) 1   2   3   (major leak).

List three things you will **do** each day to reduce this energy drain.

List three ways that you will **think differently** each day to reduce this energy drain.

List three ways to **spiritually connect and tune-in** to your Source to reduce this energy drain.

List three things to **positively affirm and speak** to lessen and reduce this energy drain.

List three **additional ways to cope** with this situation to reduce this energy drain.

List three **people that will help you** reduce this energy drain and briefly describe their assistance.

Briefly describe how you plan to **"let go" and release** this energy leak from your mind.

Now circle the number which corresponds to the amount of energy you are losing after completing the exercises above for at least a month.

0 = Energy Leak is plugged   (minor energy leak)   1   2   3   (major energy leak)

CH 4: Plugging Your Energy Leaks – Friends

Briefly describe the situation, how you are losing energy, and your reasoning for rating this leak at its present level after circling a number (minor energy leak) 1   2   3 (major leak).

List three things you will **do** each day to reduce this energy drain.

List three ways that you will **think differently** each day to reduce this energy drain.

List three ways to **spiritually connect and tune-in** to your Source to reduce this energy drain.

List three things to **positively affirm and speak** to lessen and reduce this energy drain.

List three **additional ways to cope** with this situation to reduce this energy drain.

List three **people that will help you** reduce this energy drain and briefly describe their assistance.

Briefly describe how you plan to **"let go" and release** this energy leak from your mind.

Now circle the number which corresponds to the amount of energy you are losing after completing the exercises above for at least a month.

0 = Energy Leak is plugged   (minor energy leak) 1   2   3 (major energy leak)

CH 4: Plugging Your Energy Leaks – Partner/Intimate Relationships

Briefly describe the situation, how you are losing energy, and your reasoning for rating this leak at its present level after circling a number (minor energy leak) 1   2   3 (major leak).

List three things you will **do** each day to reduce this energy drain.

List three ways that you will **think differently** each day to reduce this energy drain.

List three ways to **spiritually connect and tune-in** to your Source to reduce this energy drain.

List three things to **positively affirm and speak** to lessen and reduce this energy drain.

List three **additional ways to cope** with this situation to reduce this energy drain.

List three **people that will help you** reduce this energy drain and briefly describe their assistance.

Briefly describe how you plan to **"let go" and release** this energy leak from your mind.

Now circle the number which corresponds to the amount of energy you are losing after completing the exercises above for at least a month.

0 = Energy Leak is plugged   (minor energy leak) 1   2   3 (major energy leak)

CH 4: Plugging Your Energy Leaks – Other Leaks

Briefly describe the situation, how you are losing energy, and your reasoning for rating this leak at its present level after circling a number (minor energy leak) 1   2   3 (major leak).

List three things you will **do** each day to reduce this energy drain.

List three ways that you will **think differently** each day to reduce this energy drain.

List three ways to **spiritually connect and tune-in** to your Source to reduce this energy drain.

List three things to **positively affirm and speak** to lessen and reduce this energy drain.

List three **additional ways to cope** with this situation to reduce this energy drain.

List three **people that will help you** reduce this energy drain and briefly describe their assistance.

Briefly describe how you plan to **"let go" and release** this energy leak from your mind.

Now circle the number which corresponds to the amount of energy you are losing after completing the exercises above for at least a month.

0 = Energy Leak is plugged   (minor energy leak)   1   2   3   (major energy leak)

CH 4: Comparing Past and Present Energy Leaks and Levels – Part II

After completing the previous energy leak worksheets and performing the different activities that helped to reduce leakage, complete the worksheet below in order to compare your findings with **Part I** of this worksheet. Doing this will enable you to see where you are conserving energy as well as the areas that are still leaking and in need of attention. First, circle a number in each of the boxes, which relates to the **present level** of energy leaks in a particular category. Remember, a **level "3" leak** is the largest energy drain which constantly occupies your time and attention. A **level "2"** is a moderate-level leak while a **level "1"** is the lowest type of leak which takes the least amount of your attention, time, and energy.

School	Work	Sport	Special Activity	Family	Friends	Partner	Other Leakage
3	3	3	3	3	3	3	3
2	2	2	2	2	2	2	2
1	1	1	1	1	1	1	1

After adding up all your **present-level** energy leaks and subtracting this number from 10, circle the new amount of energy tokens you have to fuel each day.

Present Energy Leak Total_____ subtracted from 10 = _____. Circle this number below.

1	2	3	4	5	6	7	8	9	10

Now, write the number representing the **present-level** energy leakage in each of the areas (0 1 2 3) and the method(s) that worked best for plugging the energy leak in each category.

School Leaks - _____(___) Family Leaks - _____(___)

Work Leaks - _____(___) Friendship Leaks - _____ (___)

Sport Leaks - _____(___) Partnership Leaks - _____(___)

Special Activity Leaks - _____ (___) Other Leaks - _____(___)

Now, compare this worksheet and the number(s) above to the previous worksheet labeled **Part I** and the number(s) that you have written from **Part I** below. Anytime you find your fuel supply is less than 7, continue to work on plugging your energy drains in those areas that are leaking the most.

Past Energy Leak Total_____ subtracted from 10 = _____. Circle this number below.

1	2	3	4	5	6	7	8	9	10

CH 4: Identifying Energy Leaks From the Past – Part A

Think back to a span of time involving approximately 1-5 years that you previously experienced. After identifying a particular time period, list any future-oriented energy leaks that you believe were draining valuable energy at this time because of fears they created. Then, list any energy leaks related to the past that you believe were draining valuable energy at this particular time. This activity will help you to identify impacting energy leaks that may still need to be released using any of the different exercises promoting greater release; this includes the intensive process-release exercises that follow this activity.

Example: Recalling energy leaks between the ages of 15-18 that may need more releasing.

Identifying future-oriented energy leaks which were present during this time.

a). Fitting in socially   b). Grade pressures   c). College acceptance   d). Body image issues

e). Unstable relationships   f). Fearing lower performance in sports, acting, or another activity

---

Identifying past energy leaks which were present during this time span.

a). Best friend moved   b). Fight with a close friend   c). Negative mental talk

d). Parents divorced   e). Experienced bullying   f). Break up with partner

1). Recalling energy leaks between the ages of ___ – ___ that may need more releasing.

Identifying future-oriented energy leaks which were present during this time.

Identifying past energy leaks which were present during this time span.

CH 4: Identifying Energy Leaks From the Past – Part B

2). Recalling energy leaks between the ages of ___ – ___ that may need more releasing.

Identifying future-oriented energy leaks which were present during this time.

Identifying past energy leaks which were present during this time span.

3). Recalling energy leaks between the ages of ___ – ___ that may need more releasing.

Identifying future-oriented energy leaks which were present during this time.

Identifying past energy leaks which were present during this time span.

As you take some time to think about each of the potential energy leaks that you have identified over different time periods, a good way to know when an energy leak from the past needs more time being released is if it creates substantial negative thoughts, feelings, and reactions while it is being remembered. Marking these larger energy leaks on your list using a symbol of your choice such as an asterisk (*) is a great way to begin the process of identifying leaks that will need more releasing time and attention, so they do not continue to drain valuable Life energies.

CH 4: Process-Release Exercises for Cleansing the Holistic Self
Intensive Version PT I

1). Make a list of the people and the accompanying situations that are causing anger, sadness, fear, resentments, and any other negative feelings and emotions because they have not been completely processed, released, and "let go" from your deeper self.

Person _____ / Situation _____   Person _____ / Situation _____

Person _____ / Situation _____   Person _____ / Situation _____

Person _____ / Situation _____   Person _____ / Situation _____

Person _____ / Situation _____   Person _____ / Situation _____

2). For each person and problematic event, take some time to write, think about, verbalize, or imagine you are speaking to that individual (living or deceased) using the following guide in order to begin the work of processing the person and situation before you proceed to the next steps, which involve release and "letting go."

a). I appreciate ____ from you because…   b). I didn't get to tell you that…

c). I miss…   d). I was hurt by ___ because…   e). I am sorry for…

f). I needed more ___ from you because…

g). I am now releasing all pain, hurt, and negativity relating to ___ and ___ because…

3). Next, slowly speak a statement like the one below to begin the process of "letting go," cleansing, and releasing all negative events, people, and memories, which create energy leaks and poisons in our soul, body, mind, and spirit. The following activity is most effective when used in a relaxed state of mind for 5-10 minutes in the morning, afternoon, and especially right before going to sleep since the deeper, powerful "being" aspect of the self is very open to suggestion when it is relaxed.

I AM fully and freely letting go and releasing everyone and every situation that has ever caused me stress, anger, pain, or discomfort in any way, and this includes ___. I also ask and give thanks for being released from everyone and any situation that I have ever caused stress, anger, or pain to in any way, and this includes ___. Thank you for Divine cleansing's perfect work dissolving negative thoughts, words, behaviors, memories, and pain of all kinds buried deep within me. Thank you for Divine healing that is now cleaning and vacuuming me inside and out in addition to cutting all the cords and attachments which link me to negative thoughts, events, people, and memories. I know and I believe I can do all things and overcome all problems through the God Power within which strengthens, helps, and heals me in every way. Thank you God I AM being cleansed, healed, and strengthened in body, mind, and spirit as every cell, tissue, and organ is restored by day and by night to greater peace, harmony, joy, health, and well-being to my highest good in God's name.

CH 4: Process-Release Exercises for Cleansing the Holistic Self
Intensive Version PT II

4). Now, imagine that all of the stress and negativity you are releasing pours into a box at your feet. Picture yourself lighting the box which creates a special healing and transmuting fire that engulfs the box of negative memories, everyone, and everything related to these events. Imagine feeling enfolded in this powerful violet-colored flame while watching everything negative within you and the box cleansed and purified in extraordinary ways.

5). After remaining in the purifying Violet Fire for a while, now take some time to imagine yourself holding the box while sitting under a Divine waterfall of light which now saturates everything including your soul, body, mind, and spirit with healing white light that energizes, renews, and restores whatever it touches.

6). Next, allow yourself to feel tremendous joy and cleansing as all negativity is being released into the ground where this unwanted energy is transformed and then replaced with Divine healing light, peace, and restoration. Then, imagine others telling you how healthy and whole you look and that is great to see you smiling, joyful, healed, and renewed.

In the same way that hitting a nail once with a hammer does not make the nail go completely through a piece of wood, the same holds true when doing process-release exercises. This means that it may take numerous sessions before completely processing and releasing certain hurtful memories. It is fine to only use steps 3-6 when doing repetitive release sessions. The good news is that using these exercises consistently over time will help to cleanse and reprogram your deeper mind and spiritual self to go about making this special purifying work happen.

7). Anytime you experience any negative thoughts and feelings related to a past hurt in between the times you are using the process-release exercise above, this is the time to use a shorter God-power statement below which will help you to continue to heal, cleanse, and change the programing slide in your deeper mind. Think or slowly speak empowering words from an affirmation like the ones below for several minutes until your negative thinking and feeling is replaced with positive thoughts and uplifting emotions. Consistently using these light-producing exercises will always overcome darkness of any kind, including darkness related to past pain and hurtful memories. You will know a painful memory has been fully released when thinking about it no longer causes any negative emotions. Repeat this exercise as needed.

Thank you God I AM being cleansed and healed individually and in my situation involving ___ so that these memories and feelings are released and resolved to my highest good and the good of everyone involved.

Thank you God for cleansing me in soul, body, mind, spirit and helping me to release all negativity related to ___ (identify the person) and resolving this situation to my highest good and the good of everyone involved in God's name.

Thank you God for healing ___ (identify the person) and myself individually and in our relationship to the highest good of everyone involved.

Thank you God I AM being cleansed, helped, and healed every day in every way.

CHAPTER 5

GENERAL STRESS GRID (Circle all that apply to you)

Physical Reactions

- Upset stomach
- Sweating palms
- Tired or exhausted
- Susceptible to illness
- Injury from fatigue
- Slower healing
- Sore muscles
- Racing heart
- Chronic pain
- Lack of sexual desire
- Over or undereating
- Insomnia
- Other _____

Emotional Reactions

- Anger
- Sadness
- Fear
- Guilt
- Overwhelmed
- Shame
- Depressed
- Frustrated
- Exhausted
- Disappointed
- Confused
- Worried
- Other _____

Causes of Stress

- Work or school
- Family issues
- Relationship
- Negative thinking
- Loss
- Breakup
- Unresolved past
- Health issues
- Moving
- Addiction
- Financial issues
- Other _____

STRESS IS... any event, interaction, or thought that causes a physical and/or emotional reaction

Positive (+) Coping Strategies

Doing/Thinking/Coping
- Exercise / massage
- Talking to others
- Writing about an issue
- Reading
- Music
- Hobby
- Humor
- Helping others
- Relaxation exercises
- Visualization
- Staying present
- Letting go / releasing
- Spirituality / prayer
- Meditation / reflection
- Monitoring thoughts
- Tai chi or qigong
- Other _____

Communication Patterns and Stress

- Passive / avoidant
- Aggressive / bullying
- Passive-aggressive
- Assertive
- Self-talk, inner thinking
- Victimology
- Overly reactive
- Aloof / disengaged
- Controlling
- Ignoring
- Interrogating
- Other _____

Negative (-) Coping Actions

- Distracting behaviors (TV, gaming, cleaning, eating, shopping, constant partying, socializing, or working)
- Avoidance behaviors ("blowing it off," excessive procrastination, sleeping, thrill seeking, Internet or phone use)
- Harmful escaping behaviors (drug and alcohol use, running away, homicidal, or suicidal behaviors)
- Other _____

CH 5: Personalize Your Stress Grid

(Inspired by Pamela Sipe)

| List Your Physical Reactions to Stress | List Your Emotional Reactions to Stress | List the Causes of Your Stress |

STRESS IS...

| List Your Positive (+) Coping Strategies | List Your Negative (-) Coping Actions |

Identify Your Communication Patterns that Increase and Decrease Stress

Chapter 5 - Stress Busting

CH 5: Detecting Hidden Stress – Stress-Busting Master Worksheet

Proper identification of stress can be challenging. Plus, there are issues lying beneath the surface that create extra stress by being linked to the main problem. Hidden issues fueling more obvious ones are not always easy to recognize so this worksheet will assist in your detection.

Indicate with an (X) the greatest source of stress in your life right now:

___School   ___Work   ___Family   ___Money Issues   ___Peers   ___Special Partner   ___Health

___Unfinished Past   ___Fear of Future (Specify)   ___Addiction   ___Special Activity

___Disability/Injury   ___Other Person   ___Special Problem   ___Unresolved Pain   ___Other

Indicate with an (X) all of your strongest feelings linked to this major source of stress.

___Disgusted   ___Sad   ___Frustrated   ___Shocked   ___Anxious   ___Ashamed   ___Guilty

___Accepting   ___Angry   ___Depressed   ___Frightened   ___Suspicious   ___Disappointed

___Fearful   ___Confused   ___Disappointed   ___Enraged   ___Lonely   ___Overwhelmed

___Exhausted   ___Worried   ___Hysterical   (Other Feelings) _____ / _____

After writing your strongest source of stress on the first line below, think about other stressors linked to this problem and how they are adding to it. Next, take time to quiet the mind in order to be more receptive to inner guidance that can provide new insights. Then, indicate each stressor's intensity as low (L), moderate (M), high (H), or very high (VH).

Strongest, Most Pressing Source of Stress

1. _____( )
2. _____( )
3. _____( )
4. _____( )
5. _____( )

Less Obvious Stressors Happening Beneath the Surface Stress That Complicate the Issue
(This may include a lack of resources, know-how, assistance, and other special circumstances.)

The worksheets that follow can help you continue your work identifying hidden stressors that are fueling your main source of stress in addition to discovering new ways to overcome them.

CH 5: Detecting Hidden Stress – Stress-Busting Worksheet I

Briefly discuss your strongest source of stress from line 1 of the pyramid list on p. 62; then, include your reason for this and circle intensity level of this stress (i.e., low, moderate, high, very high).

List and rank your feelings linked to this stressor from 5-1 (1 = lowest stressful feeling).

5.   4.   3.   2.   1.

List what you did previously to help reduce this stress including all doing, thinking, and coping behaviors. Put a (+) next to the point if it helped and put a (-) next to the point if it did not help.

Now make a new list of all the actions you can **"do"** to help reduce this stress. Put a (+) next to the point if it helped the situation and put a (-) next to the point if it did not help.

Make a new list of all the **"thinking"** changes you can do to help reduce this stress. Put a (+) next to the point if it helped the situation and put a (-) next to the point if it did not help.

Make a new list of all the **"coping"** behaviors you can do to help reduce this stress. Put a (+) next to the point if it helped the situation and put a (-) next to the point if it did not help.

Make a new list of all the **people who can help** you reduce this stress and then note what they can do to assist. Put a (+) if they helped the situation and put a (-) if they did not help.

CH 5: Detecting Hidden Stress – Stress-Busting Worksheet II

Briefly discuss your strongest sub-stressor from line 2 of the pyramid list on p. 62; then, include your reason for this and circle intensity level of this stress (i.e., low, moderate, high, very high).

List and rank your feelings linked to this stressor from 5-1 (1 = lowest stressful feeling).

5.   4.   3.   2.   1.

List what you did previously to help reduce this stress including all doing, thinking, and coping behaviors. Put a (+) next to the point if it helped and put a (-) next to the point if it did not help.

Now make a new list of all the actions you can **"do"** to help reduce this stress. Put a (+) next to the point if it helped the situation and put a (-) next to the point if it did not help.

Make a new list of all the **"thinking"** changes you can do to help reduce this stress. Put a (+) next to the point if it helped the situation and put a (-) next to the point if it did not help.

Make a new list of all the **"coping"** behaviors you can do to help reduce this stress. Put a (+) next to the point if it helped the situation and put a (-) next to the point if it did not help.

Make a new list of all the **people who can help** you reduce this stress and then note what they can do to assist. Put a (+) if they helped the situation and put a (-) if they did not help.

CH 5: Detecting Hidden Stress – Stress-Busting Worksheet III

Briefly discuss your next strongest sub-stressor from line 3 of the pyramid list on p. 62; then, include your reason for this and circle intensity level of this stress (i.e., low, moderate, high, very high).

List and rank your feelings linked to this stressor from 5-1 (1 = lowest stressful feeling).

5.   4.   3.   2.   1.

List what you did previously to help reduce this stress including all doing, thinking, and coping behaviors. Put a (+) next to the point if it helped and put a (-) next to the point if it did not help.

Now make a new list of all the actions you can **"do"** to help reduce this stress. Put a (+) next to the point if it helped the situation and put a (-) next to the point if it did not help.

Make a new list of all the **"thinking"** changes you can do to help reduce this stress. Put a (+) next to the point if it helped the situation and put a (-) next to the point if it did not help.

Make a new list of all the **"coping"** behaviors you can do to help reduce this stress. Put a (+) next to the point if it helped the situation and put a (-) next to the point if it did not help.

Make a new list of all the **people who can help** you reduce this stress and then note what they can do to assist. Put a (+) if they helped the situation and put a (-) if they did not help.

CH 5: Detecting Hidden Stress – Stress-Busting Worksheet IV

Briefly discuss your next strongest sub-stressor from line 4 of the pyramid list on p. 62; then, include your reason for this and circle intensity level of this stress (i.e., low, moderate, high, very high).

List and rank your feelings linked to this stressor from 5-1 (1 = lowest stressful feeling).

5.   4.   3.   2.   1.

List what you did previously to help reduce this stress including all doing, thinking, and coping behaviors. Put a (+) next to the point if it helped and put a (-) next to the point if it did not help.

Now make a new list of all the actions you can "**do**" to help reduce this stress. Put a (+) next to the point if it helped the situation and put a (-) next to the point if it did not help.

Make a new list of all the "**thinking**" changes you can do to help reduce this stress. Put a (+) next to the point if it helped the situation and put a (-) next to the point if it did not help.

Make a new list of all the "**coping**" behaviors you can do to help reduce this stress. Put a (+) next to the point if it helped the situation and put a (-) next to the point if it did not help.

Make a new list of all the **people who can help** you reduce this stress and then note what they can do to assist. Put a (+) if they helped the situation and put a (-) if they did not help.

CH 5: Detecting Hidden Stress – Stress-Busting Worksheet V

Briefly discuss your weakest sub-stressor from line 5 of the pyramid list on p. 62; then, include your reason for this and circle intensity level of this stress (i.e., low, moderate, high, very high).

List and rank your feelings linked to this stressor from 5-1 (1 = lowest stressful feeling).

5.   4.   3.   2.   1.

List what you did previously to help reduce this stress including all doing, thinking, and coping behaviors. Put a (+) next to the point if it helped and put a (-) next to the point if it did not help.

Now make a new list of all the actions you can **"do"** to help reduce this stress. Put a (+) next to the point if it helped the situation and put a (-) next to the point if it did not help.

Make a new list of all the **"thinking"** changes you can do to help reduce this stress. Put a (+) next to the point if it helped the situation and put a (-) next to the point if it did not help.

Make a new list of all the **"coping"** behaviors you can do to help reduce this stress. Put a (+) next to the point if it helped the situation and put a (-) next to the point if it did not help.

Make a new list of all the **people who can help** you reduce this stress and then note what they can do to assist. Put a (+) if they helped the situation and put a (-) if they did not help.

CH 5: Releasing Physical and Emotional Pain Through Acupoint Stimulation – Part I

Previous exercises helped you to identify different sources of stress that need to be released. Using this activity, you will use the tips of your fingers to tap on different acupressure areas noted below which will help you to release physical, mental, and emotional pain as well as hurtful memories by taking the sting out of them.

1. You may use one or two hands to tap the acupoints on either or both sides of the body; however, I have found the best results from using two-hand alternate tapping on a particular point, which means I most often use a right-hand tap followed by a left-hand tap again and again, rather than tapping with both hands at the same time.

2. While you are tapping each of the acupoints (10-15 times in each area before moving onto the next acupoint), preferably speak or think to yourself a personalized version of the God-power statement below throughout the entire process in order to facilitate a powerful release of the intrusive memory and any accompanying pain.

I AM fully and freely releasing all anger, resentment, sadness, fear, negative thoughts, emotions, body pain, and/or nightmares leftover from...(name a specific stressful event), and I AM replacing all pain and hurt with Divine healing light, peace, acceptance, forgiveness, and resolution made manifest now in God's name.

3. To prepare for the activity, begin by using a version of the God-power statement above while tapping your **Upper Chest (UC)** repeatedly in a circular clockwise direction 10-15 times. Then, tap the acupoints below in the following order and way to promote a release of the physical and/or emotional pain you are experiencing.

a. Side of Hand (SH) – This point is located lengthwise on the side of each hand where a karate chop would strike an object. Tap 10-15 times on the left side of the hand, then tap 10-15 times on the right side of the hand.

b. Back of Hand (BH) – This point is located lengthwise on the back of each hand between the little finger and ring finger. Tap 10-15 times on the back of the left hand, then tap 10-15 times on the back of the right hand.

c. Webbing of Hand (WH) – This point is located on the back webbing area of each hand between the thumb and first finger. Tap 10-15 times on the back webbing of the left hand, then tap 10-15 times on the back webbing of the right hand.

d. Top of the Head (TH) – This point is located directly on the top of the head. Use alternating tapping with a right-hand tap followed by a left-hand tap repeatedly for 10-15 taps with each hand.

e. Inner Eyebrows (IB) – This point is located on the inner part of each eyebrow. Use alternating tapping with a right-hand tap followed by a left-hand tap repeatedly for 10-15 taps with each hand.

f. Side of the Eyes (SE) – This point is located on the outer bone that surrounds each eye. Use alternating tapping with a right-hand tap followed by a left-hand tap repeatedly for 10-15 taps with each hand.

g. Under the Eyes (UE) – This point is located on the bone just below each eye. Use alternating tapping with a right-hand tap followed by a left-hand tap repeatedly for 10-15 taps with each hand.

h. Under the Nose (UN)   This point in the mustache area is located under the nose and above the top lip. Use alternating tapping with a right-hand tap followed by a left-hand tap repeatedly for 10-15 taps with each hand.

i. On the Chin (OC) – This point is located under the bottom lip. Use alternating tapping with a right-hand tap followed by a left-hand tap repeatedly for 10-15 taps with each hand.

j. Collar Bone (CB) – This point is located just under the collarbone to the left and to the right of where a man would make the knot for a tie. Use alternating tapping with a right-hand tap followed by a left-hand tap on both areas repeatedly for 10-15 taps with each hand.

k. Under the Arms (UA) – This point is located on both sides of the body about 4-5 inches underneath the armpit. To reach this spot, you may choose to use a front hug of the body which means the right hand is tapping the left side of the body and the left hand is tapping the right side of the body. Use alternating tapping with a right-hand tap followed by a left-hand tap repeatedly for 10-15 taps with each hand.

l. Side of Hand (SH) – This point is located lengthwise on each side of the hand where a karate chop would strike an object. Keeping your hands about 12 inches apart, use alternating tapping with 2 right-hand taps followed by 2 left-hand taps repeatedly for 10-15 taps with each hand. Allow your eyes to follow each tap.

m. Back of Hand (BH) – This point is located lengthwise on the back of each hand between the little finger and ring finger. Keeping your hands about 12 inches apart, use alternating tapping with 2 right-hand taps followed by 2 left-hand taps repeatedly for 10-15 taps with each hand. Allow your eyes to follow each tap.

n. Webbing of Hand (WH) – This point is located on the back webbing area of each hand between the thumb and first finger. Keeping your hands about 12 inches apart, use alternating tapping with 2 right-hand taps followed by 2 left-hand taps repeatedly for 10-15 taps with each hand. Allow your eyes to follow each tap.

* Please note that this is the preferred way in which I have found the acupoints should be stimulated through tapping based on my experience. While I have found positive results using a God-power statement with this particular tapping sequence method, feel free to experiment with different versions of the statement and the tapping order of the points to determine what works best for you. Remember, there is no right or wrong way to doing this especially when it brings relief from all types of physical and emotional pain. Please consult Gary Craig's groundbreaking book, *The EFT Manual*, his website (www.emofree.com), and videos which further detail these techniques in an easy to understand way. A complete summary worksheet that follows will help to increase your understanding of this information.

CH 5: Releasing Physical and Emotional Pain Through Acupoint Stimulation – Part II

Acupoint Summary Grid

Upper Chest (UC) – Preparation for the exercise involves tapping repeatedly in a circular clockwise direction 10-15 times using one or two hands.

a. Side of the Hand (SH) – Tap 10-15 times on the left side of the hand, then tap 10-15 times on the right side of the hand.
b. Back of the Hand (BH) – Tap 10-15 times on the back of the left hand, then tap 10-15 times on the back of the right hand.
c. Webbing of the Hand (WH) – Tap 10-15 times on the back webbing of the left hand, then tap 10-15 times on the back webbing of the right hand.
d. Top of the Head (TH) – Now, use alternating tapping with a right-hand tap followed by a left-hand tap repeatedly for 10-15 taps with each hand.
e. Inner Eyebrow on both sides (IB) – Same as above.
f. Side of the Eye on both sides (SE) – Same as above.
g. Under the Eye on both sides (UE) – Same as above.
h. Under the Nose using both hands (UN) – Same as above.
i. On the Chin using both hands (OC) – Same as above.
j. Collar Bone points on both sides (CB) – Same as above.
k. Under the Arms on both sides (UA) – Same as above.
l. Side of the Hand (SH) – Continue alternating tapping now by using 2 right-hand taps followed by 2 left-hand taps repeatedly for 10-15 taps with each hand. Be sure to use your eyes to follow each tap you make.
m. Back of the Hand (BH) – Same as above.
n. Webbing of the Hand (WH) – Same as above.

I AM fully and freely releasing all anger, resentment, sadness, fear, negative thoughts, emotions, body pain, and/or nightmares leftover from…(name a specific stressful event), and I AM replacing all pain and hurt with Divine healing light, peace, acceptance, forgiveness, and resolution made manifest now in God's name.

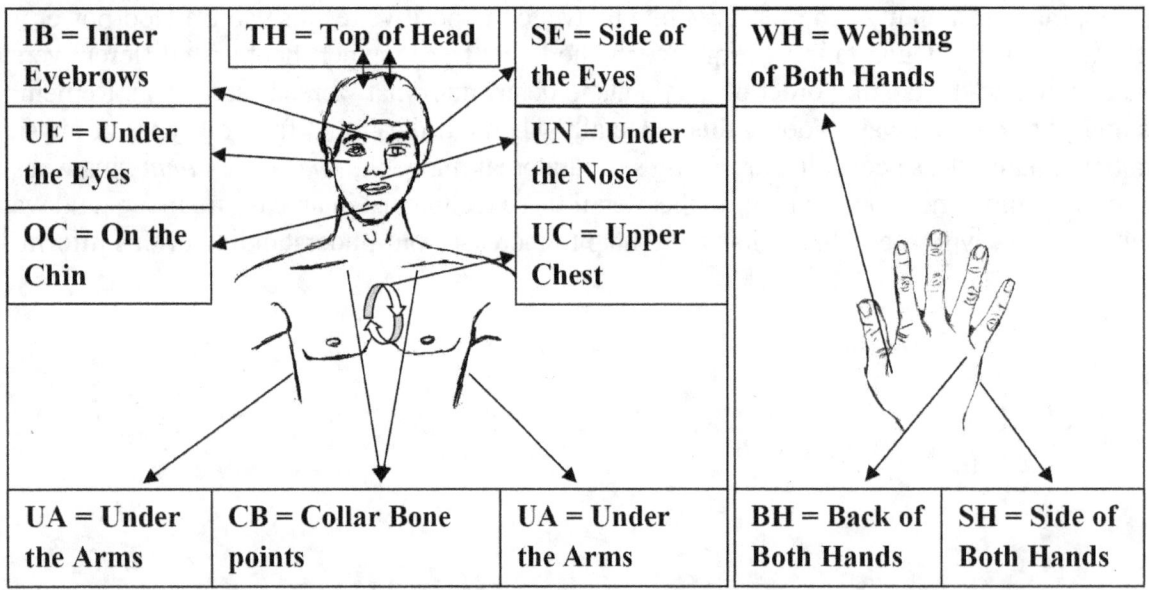

Discovering Your Excellence Within Workbook

CH 5: Examining Exercise Workout Plans – Part A

Workout Plan #1 (Includes a two-week schedule)

Sun	Mon	Tues	Wed	Thu	Fri	Sat
OFF	Upper Body + Cardio + Abs + Back Raises = (BR) + Stretching	Interval Training + Abs + (BR) + Stretching	Lower Body + Cardio + Stretching	Regular Cardio or Intervals + Abs + (BR) Stretching	Upper Body + Cardio + (BR) + Stretching	Interval Training + Abs + (BR) Stretching

Sun	Mon	Tues	Wed	Thu	Fri	Sat
OFF	Lower Body + Cardio + Back Raises = (BR) + Stretching	Interval Training + Abs + (BR) + Stretching	Upper Body + Cardio + Abs + (BR) Stretching	Regular Cardio or Intervals + Abs + (BR) Stretching	Lower Body + Cardio + (BR) + Stretching	Interval Training + Abs + (BR) + Stretching

Workout Plan #2

Sun	Mon	Tues	Wed	Thu	Fri	Sat
OFF	Upper Body + Cardio + Abs + Back Raises = (BR) + Stretching	Interval Training + Abs + (BR) + Stretching	Lower Body + Cardio + Stretching	Regular Cardio or Intervals + Abs + (BR) Stretching	Upper & Lower Body + Cardio + Stretching	Interval Training + Abs + (BR) + Stretching

Workout Plan #3

Sun	Mon	Tues	Wed	Thu	Fri	Sat
OFF	Upper & Lower Body (*) = sets or circuit training) + Cardio + Stretching	Interval Training + Abs + (BR) + Stretching	Upper & Lower Body (*) + Cardio + Stretching	Regular Cardio or Intervals + Abs + (BR) Stretching	Upper & Lower Body (*) + Cardio + Stretching	Interval Training + Abs + (BR) + Stretching

Workout Plan #4 – My Preference

Sun	Mon	Tues	Wed	Thu	Fri	Sat
OFF	Upper Body + Cardio + Abs + (BR) + Stretching	Lower Body + Cardio + (BR) + Stretching	Interval Training + Abs + (BR) + Stretching	Upper Body + Cardio + Abs + (BR) + Stretching	Lower Body + Cardio + (BR) + Stretching	Interval Training + Abs + (BR) + Stretching

CH 5: Upper Body Strength Training Exercises for Workout Plans – Part B

For each of the **upper body exercises** listed below, perform 1-3 sets of 8-12 repetitions or reps ending in or close to momentary muscular failure (MMF), which means your muscles are exhausted to the point that you cannot perform another rep. If you can only do 8 reps, the weight you are using is too heavy and doing 12 reps or more means the weight you are using is too light. Set your resistance accordingly by adding more weight, doing more reps, or by slowing down each rep especially when lowering the weight, which is the negative aspect of a repetition. Be sure to move quickly from one set to the next so that your cardio fitness improves as your muscles grow stronger. Take time to warm-up with 5-10 minutes of cardio work before doing an initial set of 15 reps with lighter weight.

1. Bench or decline press and push-ups using body weight (BW) and/or added-on weight.

2. Pullups or chin-ups (weighted or BW), inverted and bent-over rows.

3. Dips (weighted or BW), bench or chair dips, 8-second negative dips, and assisted dips.

4. Shoulder exercises include side, front, and V-raises, overhead press, and shoulder shrugs.

After completing the 4 major upper body exercises above, end with minor exercises like...

5. Tricep extensions include standing or lying down skull crushers, push-downs, and diamond push-ups, which can be performed with your knees on or off the ground.

6. Bicep curls can include single and two-arm curls as well as different variations such as a set involving lower-half curls (4 reps), upper-half curls (4 reps), and full extension curls (4 reps).

7. Abdominal work (Abs) can include front and side planks, V and leg-lift holds, hand to toe jackknives, and an array of stomach crunches. (5-7 minutes in total)

8. Back raises (BR) also known as hyperextensions or back extensions can include supermans and various back stabilizing movements using an exercise ball. (1-3 sets of 15-20 repetitions)

Straight-set training involves completing all the sets you intend to do for a specific exercise in succession before moving on to a new exercise.

In **circuit training**, you complete one set of an exercise for time (30-60 seconds) or by doing a set number of reps before moving to the next exercise, sometimes alternating upper and lower body exercises, and then repeating this total group of exercises 2-3 times during a workout.

<u>Please note that these exercises can be performed at home using body weight, hand weights, resistance bands, wearing a back pack, or by holding household items such as milk jugs or books; plus, these exercises can be readily observed using homemade or improvised strength training equipment by doing an Internet search.</u>

CH 5: Lower Body Strength Training Exercises for Workout Plans – Part C

For each of the **lower body exercises** listed below, perform 1-3 sets of 10-15 reps ending in or close to momentary muscular failure (MMF), which means your muscles are at the point where you cannot perform another repetition in good form. If you cannot do 10 reps, the weight you are using during an exercise is too heavy and if you can do 15 reps, the weight is too light. Set your resistance accordingly by adding more weight or slowing down each rep especially when lowering the weight, which is the negative aspect of a repetition. Warm-up with 5-10 minutes of cardio work before doing the routine below and strive to move as quickly as possible from one set to the next so that your cardio fitness improves as your muscles grow stronger.

1a. Lunges (forward, reverse, and side lunges), step-ups, split-leg (or runner stance) squats.

1b. Deep 2-leg deadlifts and deep 2-legged squats.

1c. One-leg Bulgarian or rear-foot elevated squats (the foot and leg not in use rests on a bench).

1d. Concentrated 1 or 2 legged squats with a ball behind your back enables sliding up and down a wall easily.

2. Wall-sits (1 and 2-legged versions, 1-5 minutes each, with 15 plyometric jumps) or leg extensions.

3. Straight-leg deadlifts (1 and 2-legged versions), good mornings, or leg curls.

4. Calf raises (three variations involving toes pointed straight, inward, and outward).

After completing the 4 major lower body exercises above, end with minor exercises like...

5. Hip flexor, abductor, and groin strengthening exercises.

6. Abdominal work (Abs) can include front and side planks, V and leg-lift holds, hand to toe jackknives, and an array of stomach crunches. (5-7 minutes in total)

7. Back raises (BR) also known as hyperextensions or back extensions can include supermans and various back stabilizing movements using an exercise ball. (1-3 sets of 15-20 repetitions)

Straight-set training involves completing all the sets you intend to do for a specific exercise in succession before moving on to a new exercise.

In **circuit training**, you complete one set of an exercise for time (30-60 seconds) or by doing a set number of reps before moving to the next exercise, sometimes alternating upper and lower body exercises, and then repeating this total group of exercises 2-3 times during a workout.

<u>Please note that these exercises can be performed at home using body weight, hand weights, resistance bands, wearing a back pack, or by holding household items such as milk jugs or books; plus, these exercises can be readily observed using homemade or improvised strength training equipment by doing an Internet search.</u>

CH 5: Cardio Exercises for Workout Plans – Part D

Regular cardio training (or just cardio for short) pertains to any physical exercises and/or movements that are sustained for at least 10 minutes of continuous effort and ideally are performed for at least 30 minutes per day preferably 5-6 days per week. Benefits of cardio training can occur through engaging in one cardio session per day, or several shorter sessions involving at least 10 minutes of sustained and continuous movement and effort. This includes, but is not limited to activities such as:

- Walking   - running   - jumping rope with or without a jump rope   - swimming

- bike riding or stationary cycling   - stair stepping or climbing   - roller or ice skating

- cross country or downhill skiing   - elliptical   - glide boarding   - numerous sports

- aerobic routines   - dancing   - hiking   - marching   - plyometric exercises

Interval Training also known as high intensity training (HIT) supersedes the benefits of regular cardio training by burning up to three times as many calories while greatly increasing cardiovascular health and the body's metabolism in the process. Similar to the effects following a strength training workout, interval training creates what is often referred to as an "after burn," which means that the body continues to burn calories efficiently for up to 48 hours following a workout and depending on the intensity level of the training.

Interval training is performed using many of the same kinds of exercises that regular cardio training uses, but the difference is that they occur at heightened levels of speed and intensity.

Example of Interval Training

Warm up for 5 minutes by doing a specific exercise, such as a stationary cycling, at a lower, slower pace that steadily increases.

During the next 15 minutes, you will perform 10 intervals in the following manner:

Go hard for 30 seconds giving an all-out effort followed by 30 seconds at a slower pace. Some people like to increase the resistance on a bike during this intense phase and then reduce the resistance during the recovery phase. These 5 one-minute intervals take 5 minutes to do, then…

Go hard for 45 seconds giving an all-out effort followed by 75 seconds at a slower pace. These 5 two-minute intervals take 10 minutes to do.

After completing the interval training above, some people will perform 5-15 minutes of regular cardio training at a lower, but steady pace.

Take 5 minutes to cool down before doing abdominal exercises, back raises and stretching.

CH 5: Daily Workout Log

UPPER BODY WORKOUT #1

DATE:	Set #1 Weight, BW/Reps (8-12)	Set #2 Weight, BW/Reps (8-12)	Set #3 Weight, BW/Reps (8-12)
Bench Press / Pushups	Bench Press _____/_____	Bench Press _____/_____	Push-Ups to Failure _____/_____
Pull-ups (+) & (-)'s / Rowing Exercises	Pull-ups / Assisted / (-)'s _____/_____	Inverted Rows (BW) Body Weight / _____	BW or Bent Over Rows _____/_____
Dips / Slow Dips / (-)'s or Bench Dips (+) & (-)'s	_____/_____	_____/_____	_____/_____
Shoulder Exercise Series (pick 4 exercises)	Side Raises _____/_____	V-Raises _____/_____	Front Raises _____/_____
	Shoulder Shrugs _____/_____	Overhead Press _____/_____	Pullovers with Dumbbell(s) _____/_____
Tricep Exercises	Pushdowns or Tricep Ext _____/_____	Tricep Skull Crushers _____/_____	Diamond Pushups _____/_____
Bicep Curls	Right Arm Curl _____/_____	Left Arm Curl _____/_____	2 Arm Curls _____/_____
Superman Back Extensions / Exercise Ball	Number of Reps to Failure	Number of Reps to Failure	Number of Reps to Failure
Ab Crunches / Planks / V's / Leg Lift Holds	Ab Crunches (4 sets) ____/____/____/____	Front & 2 Side Planks for Time ____/____/____	Timed V's / Leg Lifts _____/_____
Stretches			

UPPER BODY WORKOUT #2

DATE:	Set #1 Weight, BW/Reps (8-12)	Set #2 Weight, BW/Reps (8-12)	Set #3 Weight, BW/Reps (8-12)
Bench Press / Pushups	Bench Press _____/_____	Bench Press _____/_____	Push-Ups to Failure _____/_____
Chin-ups (+) & (-)'s / Rowing Exercises	Chin-ups / Assisted / (-)'s _____/_____	Inverted Rows (BW) Body Weight / _____	BW or Bent Over Rows _____/_____
Dips / Slow Dips / (-)'s or Bench Dips (+) & (-)'s	_____/_____	_____/_____	_____/_____
Shoulder Exercise Series (pick 4 exercises)	Side Raises _____/_____	V-Raises _____/_____	Front Raises _____/_____
	Shoulder Shrugs _____/_____	Incline or Overhead Press _____/_____	Pullovers with Dumbbell(s) _____/_____
Tricep Exercises	Pushdowns or Tricep Ext _____/_____	Tricep Skull Crushers _____/_____	Diamond Pushups _____/_____
Bicep Curls	Right Arm Curl _____/_____	Left Arm Curl _____/_____	2 Arm (Half-Half-Full Curl) _____/_____
Superman Back Extensions / Exercise Ball	Number of Reps to Failure	Number of Reps to Failure	Number of Reps to Failure
Ab Crunches / Planks / V's / Leg Lift Holds	Ab Crunches (4 sets) ____/____/____/____	Front & 2 Side Planks for Time ____/____/____	Timed V's / Leg Lifts _____/_____
Stretches			

CH 5: Daily Workout Log

LEG WORKOUT #1

DATE:	Set 1 Weight/BW/Reps (10-15)	Set 2 Weight/BW/Reps (10-15)	Set 3 Weight/BW/Reps (10-15)
Lunges	Front Lunges _____ / _____	Side Lunges _____ / _____	Reverse Lunges _____ / _____
Straight Leg Deadlifts	Right Leg Deadlifts _____ / _____	Left Leg Deadlifts _____ / _____	2 Leg Deadlifts _____ / _____
1 Leg Split Leg Squats Deep 2 Leg Deadlifts	Right Leg Split Leg Squat _____ / _____	Left Leg Split Leg Squat _____ / _____	Deep 2 Leg Deadlifts _____ / _____
Deep 2 Leg Squats Set Deep 2 Leg Deadlifts	Deep 2 Leg Squats _____ / _____	Deep 2 Leg Deadlifts _____ / _____	Deep 2 Leg Squats _____ / _____
Calf Raises	Calf Raises - Toes Straight _____ / _____	Calf Raises - Toes Inward _____ / _____	Calf Raises - Toes Outward _____ / _____
1 Leg Bulgarian Squats / Ball on Wall Squats to Failure (8 count up / down)	Right Leg Bulgarian Squats _____ / _____	Left Leg Bulgarian Squats _____ / _____	2 Leg Ball on Wall Squats _____ / _____
1 Leg Wall-Sit + 15 Plyo 2 Leg Wall-Sits + 15 Plyo	R-Leg Wall-sit / Plyo Jumps Time _____ / _____	L-Leg Wall-sit / Plyo Jumps Time _____ / _____	2 Leg Wall-sit / Plyo Jumps Time _____ / _____
Superman Back Extensions / Exercise Ball	Number of Reps to Failure	Number of Reps to Failure	Number of Reps to Failure
Ab Crunches / Planks / V's / Leg Lift Holds	Ab Crunches (4 sets) ____ / ____ / ____ / ____	Front & 2 Side Planks for Time _____ / _____ / _____	Timed V's / Leg Lifts _____ / _____
Stretches			

LEG WORKOUT #2

DATE:	Set 1 Weight/BW/Reps (10-15)	Set 2 Weight/BW/Reps (10-15)	Set 3 Weight/BW/Reps (10-15)
Lunges	Front Lunges _____ / _____	Side Lunges _____ / _____	Reverse Lunges _____ / _____
Straight Leg Deadlifts	Right Leg Deadlifts _____ / _____	Left Leg Deadlifts _____ / _____	2 Leg Deadlifts _____ / _____
Step-Ups / Split Leg Squats	Step-Ups _____ / _____	Right Leg Split Leg Squat _____ / _____	Left Leg Split Leg Squat _____ / _____
Deep 2 Leg Squats / Deep 2 Leg Deadlifts	Deep 2 Leg Squats _____ / _____	Deep 2 Leg Deadlifts _____ / _____	Deep 2 Leg Squats _____ / _____
Calf Raises	Calf Raises - Toes Straight _____ / _____	Calf Raises - Toes Inward _____ / _____	Calf Raises - Toes Outward _____ / _____
1 Leg Bulgarian (Rear-Foot Elevated) Squats to Failure	Right Leg Bulgarian Squats _____ / _____	Left Leg Bulgarian Squats _____ / _____	Your Choice _____ / _____
Ball on Wall Squats to Failure (8 count up / down)	R-Leg Ball on Wall Squats _____ / _____	L-Leg Ball on Wall Squats _____ / _____	2 Leg Ball on Wall Squats _____ / _____
Superman Back Extensions / Exercise Ball	Number of Reps to Failure	Number of Reps to Failure	Number of Reps to Failure
Ab Crunches / Planks / V's / Leg Lift Holds	Ab Crunches (4 sets) ____ / ____ / ____ / ____	Front & 2 Side Planks for Time _____ / _____ / _____	Timed V's / Leg Lifts _____ / _____
Stretches			

CH 5: Daily Workout Log

Day_____   Date_____

List Exercises: As part of a warm-up:_____minutes. As part of a cool down:_____minutes.

Cardio and Interval Exercises: Record as minutes, number of miles, or intervals completed.

Running_____   Walking_____   Elliptical_____   Glide Board_____   Rowing_____

Cycling_____   Aerobics_____   Stairclimbing_____   Other_____   Swimming_____

Strength Training Exercises:

1). Exercise Performed:_____   **2). Exercise Performed:**_____

Set 1_____Weight_____Reps:_____   Set 1_____Weight_____Reps:_____

Set 2_____Weight_____Reps:_____   Set 2_____Weight_____Reps:_____

Set 3_____Weight_____Reps:_____   Set 3_____Weight_____Reps:_____

3). Exercise Performed:_____   **4). Exercise Performed:**_____

Set 1_____Weight_____Reps:_____   Set 1_____Weight_____Reps:_____

Set 2_____Weight_____Reps:_____   Set 2_____Weight_____Reps:_____

Set 3_____Weight_____Reps:_____   Set 3_____Weight_____Reps:_____

5). Exercise Performed:_____   **6). Exercise Performed:**_____

Set 1_____Weight_____Reps:_____   Set 1_____Weight_____Reps:_____

Set 2_____Weight_____Reps:_____   Set 2_____Weight_____Reps:_____

Set 3_____Weight_____Reps:_____   Set 3_____Weight_____Reps:_____

7). Exercise Performed:_____   **8). Exercise Performed:**_____

Set 1_____Weight_____Reps:_____   Set 1_____Weight_____Reps:_____

Set 2_____Weight_____Reps:_____   Set 2_____Weight_____Reps:_____

Set 3_____Weight_____Reps:_____   Set 3_____Weight_____Reps:_____

9). Abdominal Exercises: Sets/Reps_____   **10). Back Raises:** Sets/Reps_____

_____: Sets/Reps_____   _____: Sets/Reps_____

CH 5: Memory Cleansing Exercise Before Sleeping – Part I

1). Just before bedtime, use the following memory cleansing exercise to remove the layers of emotional pain and hurt while we sleep, since this will enable us to be more peaceful, happy, and healed individuals. Each night we use these words, we are making a deposit into our special bank account that will provide a fantastic return of our time and energies by filling us with Divine healing light while taking the sting out of any hurtful memories.

Thank you for Divine cleansing entering deeply into my mind and memory today and especially as I rest. Every hurt that has ever been done to me, please heal those injuries. All the negative things that I have ever done to others, please heal those injuries. All relationships in my life that have been damaged that I am aware of and unaware of, please heal those errors. If anyone is still suffering from my thoughts, words, and actions, please bring those people to my awareness, so I can make things right. I choose to let go and forgive others, and I ask to be released and forgiven too. Thank you for Divine restoration's perfect work healing and cleansing me of all sickness, injury, disease, discord, and error including all negative thoughts, words, actions, or curses directed toward me, released by me, or held within me especially involving ____. Thank you for Divine love's perfect work removing all bitterness, anger, sadness, fear, resentment, negative emotions, and painful memories within my body, mind, spirit, and heart especially involving ____. Thank you for replacing all negativity and darkness within me with Divine healing light, acceptance, forgiveness, compassion, and peaceful resolution in God's name, Amen.

2). Now take some time to imagine sitting under a beautiful, cleansing waterfall of Divine white light that is raining down tremendous healing, peace, and restoration upon you and the issues needing release. Then, picture and feel the uplifting emotions and feelings you will experience as all negativity, pain, hurt, and injuries are washed away and replaced with Divine healing light and its heightened spiritual energy. Be sure to breathe in deeply all aspects of this remarkable healing light and then expel all unwanted energy with every breath you exhale.

3). Next, imagine the significant people in your life telling you how healthy and whole you look and that it is great to see you happy, peaceful, energized, and renewed. Make this image as real and tangible as possible by closely observing every aspect that is involved. Take time to feel all of the emotions and sensations linked to these events and the people in your life. Be sure to listen to all of the sounds related to this experience as well as what these people are saying to you. Note any smells or tastes that may be present particularly if the scene is taking place around the beach or a banquet type of setting where food is being served.

4). Doing these exercises daily will help to cleanse all aspects of the self while reprograming your deeper mind and spiritual self to go about making it happen. Over time, this cleansing exercise will help to remove all negative emotions by taking the sting out of any painful memories that are still impacting and hurtful. Your main task is to be consistent in practicing these exercises each and every day because practicing is related to positive outcomes.

CH 5: Memory Cleansing Exercise Before Sleeping – Part II

5). During the day, anytime you happen to experience any negative feelings from hurtful thoughts and memories that continue to surface, use a shorter God-power statement below or one of your own making that will continue to help you heal, cleanse, and change the slides of your deeper mind. It is best to use the shorter God-power statements below in combination with deeper breathing for several minutes by silently thinking or speaking these enriching words slowly until your negative thinking and feelings are replaced with Divine light, positive thinking and feelings, and increased peace. In time, the higher energy and special healing light that you are releasing from using these exercises consistently throughout the day will always overcome darkness of any kind. Repeat this exercise as often as necessary.

Thank you God I AM being helped and healed individually and in my relationship with ___ (person's name) so that any painful memories are released and resolved to my highest good and the good of everyone involved.

Thank you God for helping and healing ___ (person's name) and myself individually and in our relationship and for resolving this situation involving ___ to my highest good and the good of everyone involved.

Thank you God for cleansing me in body, mind, spirit and helping me release all negative thoughts and hurtful memories while healing me and ___ (person's name) individually and in this situation to our highest good.

Thank you God I AM being helped and healed every day in every way.

Thank you I AM filled with Divine light, peace, and healing because if God is with me, who or what can be against me?

Now, take some time to write several positive affirmations of your own that you can readily use whenever you are feeling stressed or being bombarded by negative emotions of all kinds.

CH 5: Summary of "Go To" Strategies for Overcoming Stress

(Inspired by Marvin)

A. Visualize a Wave and Use Leg Taps for a Past or Future Focus	B. Play, Hum, Listen to, or Sing Some Music Out Loud or in Your Mind	C. Set an Intention Before Doing Anything to Avoid Self-Sabotage	D. Use Affirmations, I AM…and God-Power Statements Regularly
E. Use Deep Breathing with Imagery: Inhale Light–Exhale Darkness	F. Use Movement, Workouts, and Exercise to Feel Better (Includes Walking a Pet)	G. Do Process and Release Exercises with Tapping Points to "Let It Go"	H. Practice Longer Tune-Ins, Prayers and Inspirational Reading
I. Notice Negative (-) Feeling Alerts to Adjust Thoughts, Words, and Actions	J. Examine and Change Negative (-) Thoughts Using a Diamond ♦ Thinking Worksheet	K. Make an Attitude of Gratitude List Each Day	L. Work on Staying in the Present Now; Then Get into "the Zone"
M. Talk Out Your Stress with Others, Pets, or Your Source	N. Use Healing Imagery and Visualization to Cleanse and Renew in Your Special Place	O. Write Out Your Stress in a Journal, Poem, or Song	P. Practice Random or Calculated Acts of Kindness
Q. Use Relaxation Methods Like Tense and Flood Techniques (TFT)	R. Get a Hobby, Read, Create Some Art, Music, a Book, or Do Something Useful	S. Try to Find Humor in an Event and Laugh at It	T. Practice Open, Honest, and Assertive Communication
U. Get or Give a Hug, Neck or Palm Rub, Full Massage, or Take a Bath	V. Use a Problem-Solving Worksheet to Find Options and Resolve Challenges	W. Spend Time in a Garden or Nature Doing Some Fun Activities	X. Turn Any and All Difficulties Over to Your Source
Y. Avoid Negative People and Spend Time with Uplifting Ones	Z. Practice Being Still Using Meditation, Qigong, Tai Chi, or Other Reflective Practices	ZZ. Realize We Do Not Control All Experiences, Only Self and Our Reactions	ZZZ. Your Choice:

For each day of the week, write the letters from the chart above for the strategies that you used to bring greater peace into your life while reducing your stress and negative thinking in the process. Doing this will help you to see all of the ways that you use to better cope with the challenges you experience.

Monday	
Tuesday	
Wednesday	
Thursday	
Friday	
Saturday	
Sunday	

CHAPTER 6
Daily Checklist for Keeping High Vibes

___ Workout or exercise for at least 30 minutes per day and 10-minute sessions work well too.
___ Use massage to release tension and pain through neck, back, palm, and feet rubs.
___ Use hot showers and baths to relax and renew.
___ Practice deep breathing with no thinking at all.
___ Strive for 7-8 hours of sleep per night.
___ Consume a healthy Mediterranean diet that includes ample servings of fruit and vegetables.
___ Limit your intake of junk and processed food.
___ Limit your use of prescription medication if possible.
___ Avoid or limit the use of alcohol.
___ Avoid recreational drug use.
___ Listen to high vibe music while avoiding songs with negative or aggressive lyrics.
___ Limit your use of television, movie watching, and computer games and particularly those with negative, aggressive, prejudicial, or violent themes, language, and behaviors.
___ Avoid excessive use of the Internet, social media sites, and texting.
___ Use caution/protection with microwave ovens, computers, cell phones, other technologies.
___ Seek jobs that uplift energy and promote healthy work environments and practices.
___ Include positive humor and laughter daily, but never at another's expense.
___ Take "me" time to relax and recharge by doing nothing.
___ Take time for fun activities, interests, hobbies, and volunteering.
___ Be aware when your mind-talk becomes negative and replace it with positive affirmations.
___ If you find yourself in a lower mood, do something different and change your thinking.
___ Stay in the present moment for higher energy, mindfulness, and "the zone" experiences.
___ Notice and adjust oscillating thoughts that move from past to future with no present focus.
___ Keep a peaceful mindset by playing an uplifting song in your thoughts.
___ Use relaxation and visualization techniques, deep breathing, and stretching to renew energy.
___ Perform random and calculated acts of kindness for those you know and do not know.
___ Practice the "golden rule" (think, act, and speak to others as you want them to do unto you).
___ Connect to Source Energy consistently through prayer, reflection, and quiet meditation.
___ Engage in inspirational reading and encourage this in others.
___ Turn over problems and difficulties to your Higher Power for easier resolution.
___ Practice life-long learning for intellectual stimulation and encourage others to do the same.
___ Promote uplifting conversations with friends, family, your partner, and acquaintances.
___ Communicate in writing when you have limited or no verbal interaction with people.
___ Limit contact with negative and lower vibratory influences, including certain people.
___ Work to continually release and "let go" of past hurts, situations, and those who offend you.
___ Try to be the change that you wish to see in the world each and every day.
___ For best results, be consistent when doing the above practices.

CH 6: Keeping High Vibes – Examining Consumables

1. List the low-vibe foods, such as most processed and packaged foods and particularly those with high fat or sugar-content, you would like to minimize or avoid and briefly explain why.

List the new high-vibe foods, such as all kinds of vegetables, fruits, nuts, and whole-grain foods, that are healthy substitutes.

2. List the low-vibe drinks, such as soda pop and most energy drinks, you would like to minimize or avoid and briefly explain why.

List the new high-vibe drinks, such as water, tea, and coffee, which are healthy substitutes.

3. List other low-vibe and/or harmful substances, such as tobacco products, alcohol, and various types of drugs, you would like to minimize or avoid and briefly explain why.

List the new high-vibe substances and/or replacements that are healthy substitutes.

4. List some bullet (-) points that can promote positive changes to the categories below.

Food	Drinks	Other Substances

CH 6: Keeping High Vibes – Examining Things You Do

1. List the low-vibe and/or harmful activities you would like to minimize or avoid and briefly explain why.

List the new high-vibe activities that are healthy substitutes.

2. List the low-vibe hobbies you would like to minimize or avoid and briefly explain why.

List the new high-vibe hobbies that are healthy substitutes.

3. List other low-vibe and/or harmful interests you would like to minimize or avoid and briefly explain why.

List the new high-vibe interests and/or replacements that are healthy substitutes.

4. List some bullet (-) points that can promote positive changes to the categories below.
Activities   Hobbies   Interests

CH 6: Keeping High Vibes – Examining Where You Spend Time

1. List the low-vibe places, which are energy depleting, negative, and/or depressing because of what occurs there, that you would like to minimize or avoid and briefly explain why.

List the new high-vibe places that are healthy and uplifting substitutes.

2. List the low-vibe organizations, such as groups that demean, insult, and discriminate against others, that you would like to minimize or avoid and briefly explain why.

List the new high-vibe organizations that are healthy and uplifting substitutes.

3. List other low-vibe and/or harmful environments, such as settings promoting violence, pollution, and injustice, that you would like to minimize or avoid and briefly explain why.

List the new high-vibe environments and/or replacements that are healthy, uplifting substitutes.

4. List some bullet (-) points that can promote positive changes to the categories below.
Places   Organizations   Environments

CH 6: Keeping High Vibes – Examining the Company You Keep

1. List the challenging acquaintances and colleagues that you would like to minimize or avoid contact with and briefly explain.

List the uplifting acquaintances and colleagues that you would like to spend more time with and briefly explain why.

2. List the challenging friends that you would like to minimize or avoid contact with and briefly explain why.

List the uplifting friends that you would like to spend more time with and briefly explain why.

3. List the challenging family members and relatives that you would like to minimize or avoid contact with and briefly explain why.

List the uplifting family members and relatives that you would like to spend more time with and briefly explain why.

4. List some bullet (-) points that can promote positive changes to the categories below.

Acquaintances	Colleagues	Friends	Family Members

CH 6: Keeping High Vibes – Summary of Contributors to Energy Lows and Highs

List the things you need to minimize or avoid because they often take your energy down.

List the things you can do to help keep your energy high.

List the people in your life that can help you keep your energy high.

CHAPTER 7
Example of a Negative Thinking Worksheet – Part I

While the ideas in the example below teach how a negative mindset can lead to positive thinking changes, everyone personalizes these thoughts in his or her own special way.

1. Describe a negative situation that happened to you.

During a competitive sporting event, I experienced a mediocre performance that caused a lot of negative thinking and a loss of confidence. This was very upsetting and something I do not want to experience again, so I am eager to learn about different ways to avoid this from happening in the future.

2. Write your negative (stress-producing) thoughts and beliefs about the situation:

How can I keep making the same mistakes? I'm so dumb.

I will probably lose my position, respect, or maybe even get kicked off the team if this keeps happening.

If I keep making mistakes, I do not think that I'll ever be good enough to participate at a higher level.

My teammates, coach, parents, friends, and the fans will be disappointed even if they try hard not to show it.

3. Write your negative feelings about the situation.

I feel angry, sad and depressed, and low on energy when things like this happen to me.

I feel like I'm going to be a failure and life-long loser who will never excel at higher levels.

I feel like I don't have the confidence I once had.

Lower performances sometimes make me feel like I just want to quit.

4. Write any negative behaviors that are occurring as a result of the situation.

Sometimes I don't give my best effort because I don't want to risk disappointment.

Sometimes I fake illness or injury so I have an excuse when I do not excel.

Sometimes I like to numb my pain with substances that make me feel better.

I find myself criticizing other people more often for their shortcomings and lower performance.

CH 7: Example of a Negative Thinking Worksheet – Part II

5. How did your inner mind-talk make the situation worse?

Once the negative thinking began, it was difficult to get it to stop for any period of time because these thoughts would come back again and again.

I kept telling myself that I would probably make more mistakes, and that I would never accomplish my long-term goals and desires.

The more negative thoughts I had about the situation, the worse this made me feel.

Over time, my negative thinking which led to lower feelings also resulted in poorer behaviors.

6. Confronting the negative thoughts and beliefs. Write some new and different thoughts which you could have chosen that would have helped the situation and your negative thinking.

Hey, one mistake does not mean that I'm a failure or my season and career are doomed, so I need to relax and go easier on myself.

I will talk to the coach and other friends on the team to get some extra tips and practice that will help address this situation and make me better.

None of my friends are perfect as they make mistakes too, just like me.

I think everything will turn out fine as I start using my new resources and power!

7. Write the new feelings that result from this improved thinking.

I feel a lot more confident now that I'm not insulting myself with negative thinking.

I feel a big weight has been lifted by "letting go" of negative thoughts, so I feel much more energized and joyful too.

I feel my future is bright when I problem-solve rather than dwelling on what is past and painful and cannot be undone.

My new-found confidence provides a much more peaceful state of mind before, during, and after events.

CH 7: Example of a Negative Thinking Worksheet – Part III

8. Write the new behaviors that result from improved thinking.

I am much more focused now and in control of my life and my career, so I can't wait to compete.

I want to work on becoming a leader and showing my teammates how to keep a positive mindset since this has worked so well for me.

I also want to help teach youngsters how to problem-solve and use the tools that I had to learn the hard way.

I find my use of God-power statements like, "Thank you God I AM filled with all the strength, confidence, and skills I need to succeed as Divine guidance and protection helps me in all ways," releases all kinds of amazing benefits that are always accessible and available.

9. What other scenarios could have occurred with different thinking?

I could have experienced a lot less stress and misery if I had addressed my thinking sooner and more effectively by using this kind of exercise. I also could have experienced success much sooner and with a more peaceful mindset if I had corrected my thinking and then addressed the problems by "doing" what I needed to in order to correct and improve my performance.

10. Write down any final thoughts about how this exercise can impact your future.

I plan to be much more proactive in the future by confronting my negative thinking immediately and changing this by using power words and phrases, positive affirmations, and God-power statements which together will enable me to think, feel, and act from the highest that is within me. Using this type of exercise gives me the tools and the confidence to overcome any problem because so much of the stress relates to how we think about it.

CH 7: Negative Thinking Worksheet – Part I

1. Describe a negative situation that happened to you.

2. Write your negative (stress-producing) thoughts and beliefs about the situation.

3. Write your negative feelings about the situation.

4. Write any negative behaviors that are occurring as a result of the situation.

5. How did your inner mind-talk make the situation worse?

CH 7: Negative Thinking Worksheet – Part II

6. Confronting the negative thoughts and beliefs - Write some new and different thoughts which you could have chosen that would have helped the situation and your negative thinking.

7. Write your new feelings that result from different thinking.

8. Write any new behaviors that result from different thinking.

9. What other scenarios could have occurred with different thinking?

10. Write down any final thoughts about how this exercise can impact your future.

CH 7: Diamond Thinking Worksheet

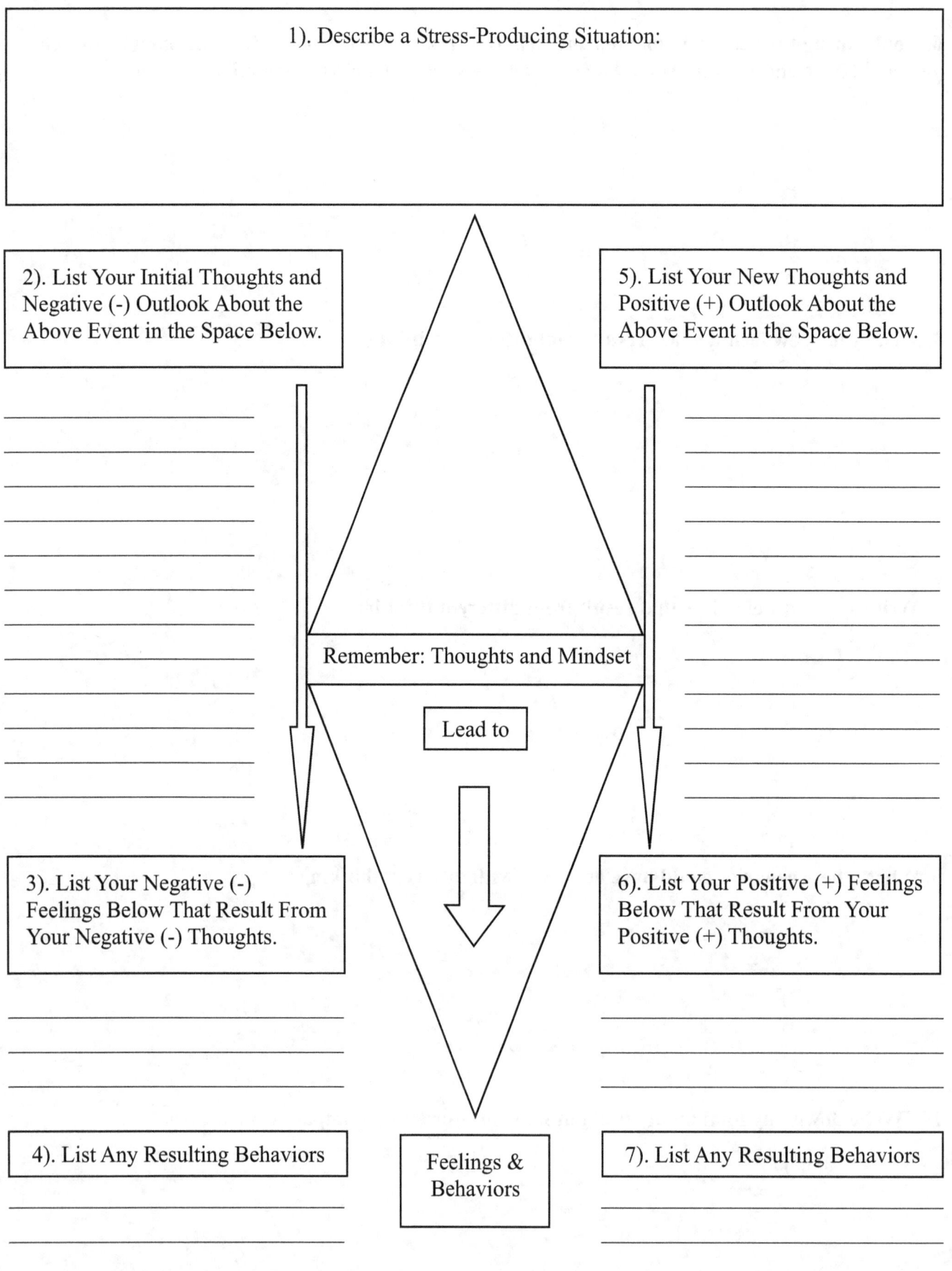

92 Discovering Your Excellence Within Workbook

CH 7: Diamond Thinking Worksheet

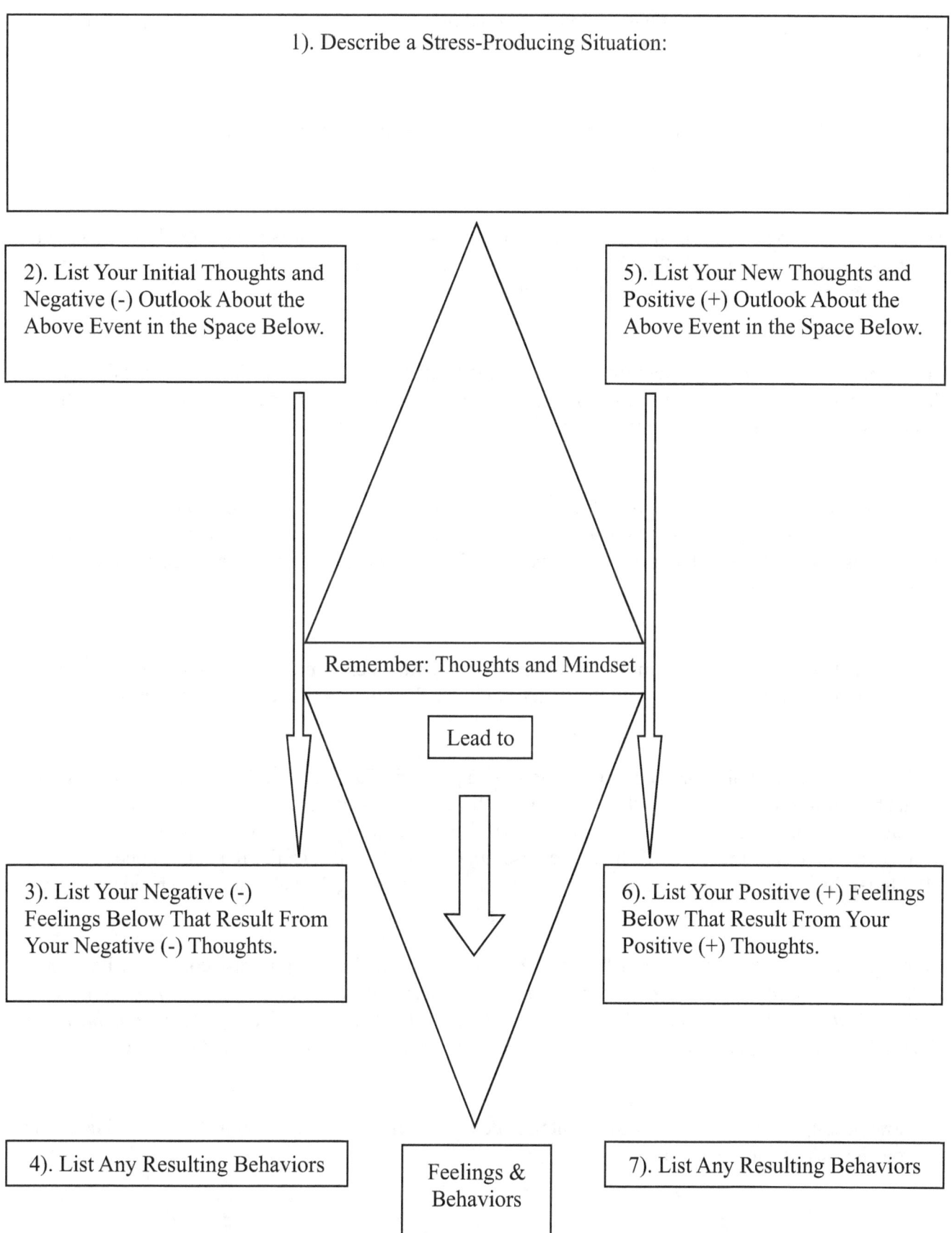

Chapter 7 - Overcoming Negative Thinking 93

CH 7: Releasing and Replacing Intrusive Past Thoughts – Part I

1). Think about a past event that has caused emotional pain and upset and continues to hurt when reflected upon.

2). Now rate this event on a scale of 1-10 with a 10 producing the most emotional pain possible and a 0 producing the least.

3). Next, as you take about 2-3 minutes to think about this past hurtful situation, you will be viewing this event, not as someone reliving the scenario, but as someone who is essentially making a video or movie of a past event that you also happened to be part of at one time.

4). Begin by imagining and visualizing what happened before (approximately 30 seconds) and then after this hurtful experience (approximately 30 seconds), before focusing on the actual event itself which should include the majority of the time and focus of about 1-2 minutes.

5). Think about as much detail as possible during this movie-making exercise and you may even find that your memory brings back additional details of the situation. Then, re-run the movie in your mind several more times while changing the order of the events in different ways (i.e., end-beginning-middle, end-middle-beginning, middle-beginning-end).

6). Now that you made a mental movie of this event, place this mental movie reel in an imaginary box for the moment as you think about all that you have learned from this challenging experience.

7). Next, use the Acupoint Tapping Exercise found on pages 68-70 of this workbook to tap on these points beginning with circular clockwise taping of the upper chest followed by: 1). Side of the hands 2). Back of the hands 3). Webbing of the hands 4). Top of the head 5). On the inner eyebrows 6). Side of the eyes 7). Under the eyes 8). Under the nose 9). On the chin 10). Under the collar bones 11). Under the arms 12). Side of the hands 13). Back of the hands 14). Webbing of the hands.

8). As you are tapping each of the different acupoints, repeat the following phrase continuously: *I AM fully and freely releasing all anger, resentment, sadness, fear, negative thoughts, emotions, body pain, and/or nightmares leftover from…(name this stressful event), and I AM replacing all pain and hurt with Divine healing light, peace, acceptance, forgiveness, and resolution made manifest now in God's name.*

9). Now pick up the imaginary box that contains the mental movie reel that you just made and hold this on your lap with your palms up.

CH 7: Releasing and Replacing Intrusive Past Thoughts – Part II

10). For several minutes, picture the box and movie reel, the room, yourself, and everyone involved in the event engulfed in a powerful Violet Fire since this energy will cleanse and transform everything it touches in amazing ways.

11). Now take several minutes to picture to everyone and everything being soaked by a powerful waterfall of Divine white healing light which heals, renews, and restores everything it touches in amazing ways.

12). Next, put the healing of this situation in the palm of your hands and turn it over completely to your Higher Power. Whenever this returns to your mind, use positive affirmations, words or phrases, and especially God-power statements such as, *"Thank you God I AM being completely healed in body, mind, and spirit and released of any negativity and pain related to this incident made manifest now in Divine order and perfection,"* to consistently confront and change any negative thinking before it begins to engulf the mind and lead to negative emotions and upset. Making use of God-power statements throughout each day and especially when you find distressing thoughts invading your mind will also help to solidify your intention of bringing peace and resolution to challenging situations.

13). Then, rate this event again on a scale of 1-10 with a 10 producing the most emotional pain possible and a 0 producing the least to see if your negative thoughts and emotions related to these past events still need more process and release work. Any stress rating at the level of 3 or above suggests continuing in the use of this exercise, which in time, will reduce this rating to lower levels. People often find that the emotional pain they previously noted is significantly reduced because this exercise utilizes a combination of powerful healing tools that impact deeper aspects of the holistic self while releasing emotional pain and negativity in the process.

14). Be sure to repeat this exercise consistently and the use of positive or God-power statements often and especially when you find intrusive thoughts invading the mind.

CH 7: Releasing and Replacing Intrusive Future Thoughts – Part I

1). Think about an event that will happen in the near future which is causing you to experience stress, upset, fear and worry right now. Now rate this situation on a scale of 1-10 with a 10 producing the most emotional stress possible and a 0 producing the least.

2). Next, as you take about a minute to think about this stressful situation, you will be viewing this event, not as someone involved in the scenario, but as someone who is essentially making a video or movie of an event that you also happen to be part of. Begin by imagining and visualizing what may happen before (approximately 15 seconds) and then after this potentially stressful experience (approximately 15 seconds), before spending the majority of the time and focus, which is about 30 seconds, on the actual event itself.

3). Now that you made a mental movie of this stressful event, place this mental movie reel in an imaginary box as you take a few moments to think about all that you have learned so far from this challenging experience.

4). Next, use the Acupoint Tapping Exercise found on pages 68-70 of this workbook to tap on these points beginning with circular clockwise taping of the upper chest followed by: 1). Side of the hands 2). Back of the hands 3). Webbing of the hands 4). Top of the head 5). On the inner eyebrows 6). Side of the eyes 7). Under the eyes 8). Under the nose 9). On the chin 10). Under the collar bones 11). Under the arms 12). Side of the hands 13). Back of the hands 14). Webbing of the hands.

5). As you are tapping each of the different points, repeat the following phrase continuously: *I AM fully and freely releasing all anger, resentment, sadness, fear, negative thoughts, emotions, body pain, and/or nightmares related to…(name the specific stressful event), and I AM replacing all stress, pain, and worry with Divine healing light, peace, acceptance, forgiveness, and resolution made manifest now in God's name.*

6). Now place the imaginary box with the mental movie reel that you just made and hold this on your lap with your palms up.

7). For several minutes, picture the box and movie reel, the room, yourself, and everyone involved in the event engulfed in a powerful Violet Fire since this energy will cleanse and transform everything it touches in amazing ways.

CH 7: Releasing and Replacing Intrusive Future Thoughts – Part II

8). Next, take several minutes to imagine this stressful situation being totally resolved in an amazing way. Think about as much detail as possible during this movie recreating exercise by taking time to imagine what you would like to see happen before (approximately 30 seconds), during (approximately 30 seconds), and especially after this situation is completely resolved. This means that the majority of your time and focus, which is about 2-3 minutes, will be spent imagining what you and others, such as family and friends, will be experiencing and feeling after this positive outcome occurs.

9). Now take several minutes to imagine everyone associated with the event being soaked by a powerful waterfall of Divine white healing light which heals, renews, and resolves everything it touches in amazing ways.

10). Next, put this situation in the palm of your hands and turn it over completely to your Higher Power. Whenever this event returns to your mind, use a positive affirmation, power word or phrase, and especially God-power statements such as, *"Thank you God for resolving this situation in Divine order and perfection and for helping and healing everyone involved to our highest good,"* to consistently confront fearful, negative, and worrisome thinking before it becomes intrusive and solidifies within the mind and your world. Also, be sure to continually remind yourself that turning this problem over to your Source means that it is in the best hands.

11). Take a moment to rate this stressful event again on a scale of 1-10 with a 10 producing the most emotional stress possible and a 0 producing the least to see if your negative thoughts and emotions related to these future events still need more process and release work. Any stress rating at the level of 3 or above suggests continuing in the use of this exercise, which in time, will reduce this rating to lower levels.

12). Be sure to practice the visualized scenes in steps 7-9 at least twice a day and especially when you first wake up and just before sleeping at night. Making use of God-power statements like the one in step 10 throughout each day and especially when you find distressing thoughts invading your mind will help to solidify your intention of bringing peace and resolution to challenging situations. As you do this, many people find that their stressful thoughts are significantly reduced upon completion of these exercises because this combination of powerful healing tools impacts deeper aspects of the holistic self while releasing fear, worry, and negativity in the process.

13). Remember to repeat this exercise consistently and the use of positive or God-power statements often and especially when you find intrusive thoughts about future events invading your mind.

CHAPTER 8
Using Thoughts to Create Constructively – Part I

Describe in detail what you would like to be, create for yourself, or overcome. Include every aspect of what you want to be doing, feeling, and experiencing.

Important Reminders:
   a. FOCUS YOUR ATTENTION regularly on what you want rather than focusing on what you do not want or what you fear because ***energy follows mental focus and attention***.
   b. BEING AWARE of what you allow your mind to dwell upon means MONITORING your thoughts constantly so you DO NOT create what you don't want.
   c. When you start to FEEL BADLY, this is a SIGNAL that your thinking is negative. REPLACE this thinking immediately so it DOES NOT begin the process of creating problematic situations.
   d. Be sure to RELEASE all negative thoughts toward hurtful events and others each day.

Write the affirmation(s) you will use to help create your thoughts and desires.

Write the thoughts and affirmations that you will use to replace any negative feelings and thinking which you may experience during this process.

CH 8: Using Thoughts to Create Constructively – Part II

Make a list of the important things you will **do** daily to help make this desire a reality.

List the spiritual practices you will use to provide additional power and energy to create your desires.

| | a._____ | b._____ | c._____ |

When will you
do this?   a._____   b._____   c._____

Where will you
do this?   a._____   b._____   c._____

How often?   a._____   b._____   c._____

For how long?   a._____   b._____   c._____

List the people that can help you accomplish this goal and desire; then, briefly describe their help.

CH 8: Using Thoughts to Create Constructively – Part III

Plan to use at least two visualization sessions daily to help produce your goal and desire. Then, describe in detail the kind of mental imagery and visualization you will use in conjunction with your affirmations.

When will this occur?

Where will this occur?

How often?

For how long?

CH 8: Creating Life Experiences Grid

1). Describe a situation or desire that you would like to create for yourself.

2). List any negative (-) thoughts below that can prevent you from creating this situation and desire.

5). List the positive (+) thoughts below that will assist you in creating this situation and desire.

Remember: Thoughts and Mindset
+
Feelings, Time, and Attention

3). List any negative (-) feelings below that result from your negative (-) thoughts knowing these will give your thoughts the power to create.

6). List any positive (+) feelings below that result from your positive (+) thoughts knowing these will give your thoughts the power to create.

Create

4). List the negative (-) life experiences below that can result from your negative (-) thoughts and feelings.

7). List the positive (+) life experiences below that can result from your positive (+) thoughts and feelings.

Personal Life Experiences

Chapter 8 - Unleashing the Power of Thought

CH 8: Creating Life Experiences Grid

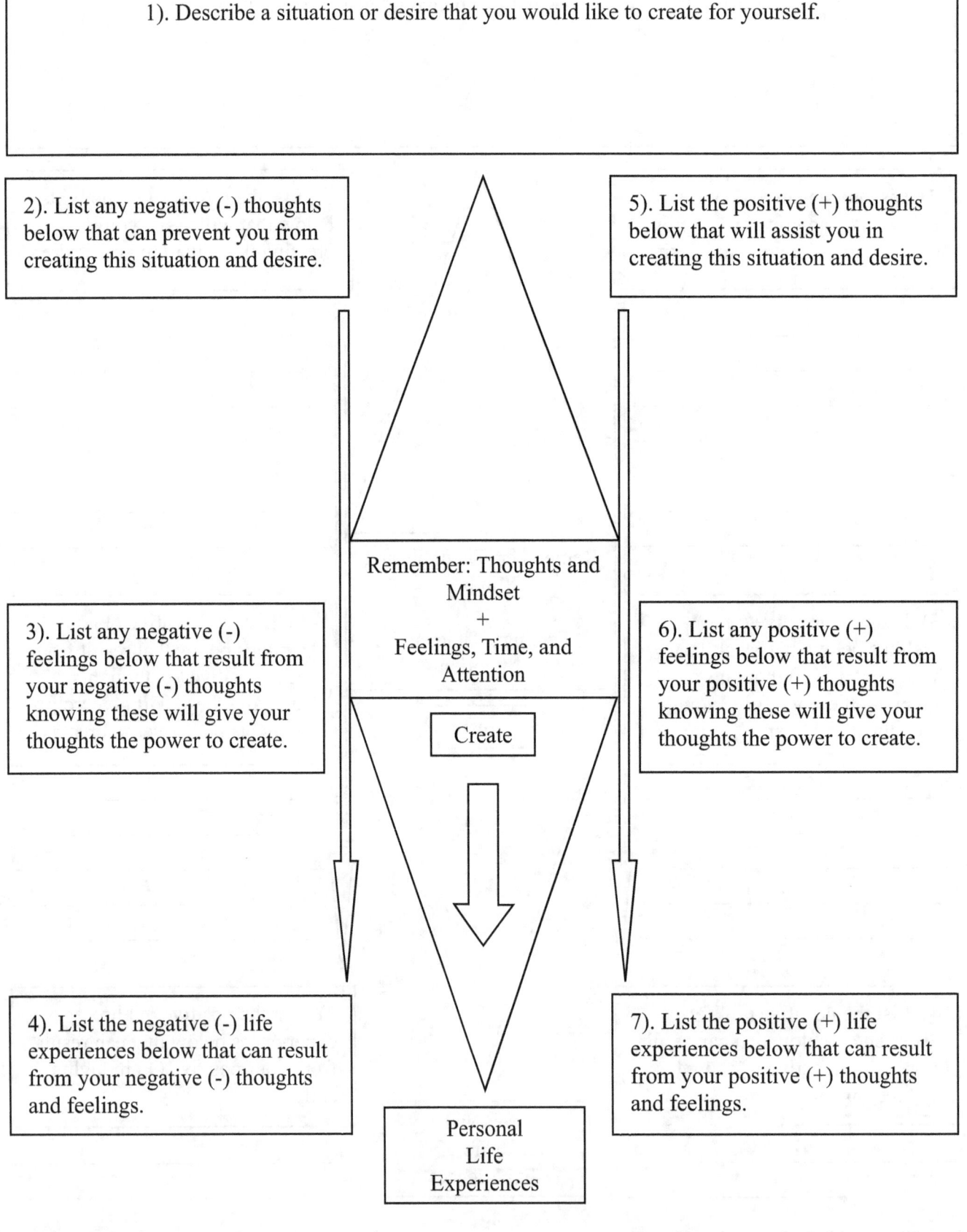

CH 8: Identifying and Overcoming Personal Mental Shadows – Part IV

1. Identify the troubling thoughts acting as scary mental shadows that are occurring in your life and mind now.

2. List some ways that you challenge and confront these troubling mental thoughts and shadows when they begin to appear.

3. Write some new thoughts and affirmations you will use to challenge and overcome the scary mental thinking shadows you are facing.

4. List some ways that you will process and release the scary mental shadows you are facing. Processing may include talking, writing or thinking about the event, and then releasing it into a waterfall of Divine light, Violet Fire imagery, or any other method you prefer.

Important Reminders:
   a. FOCUS YOUR ATTENTION regularly on what you want rather than focusing on what you do not want or what you fear because ***energy follows mental focus and attention***.
   b. BEING AWARE of what you allow your mind to dwell upon means MONITORING your thoughts constantly so you DO NOT create what you don't want.
   c. When you start to FEEL BADLY, this is a SIGNAL that your thinking is negative. REPLACE this thinking immediately so it DOES NOT begin the process of creating problematic situations.
   d. Be sure to RELEASE all negative thoughts toward hurtful events and others each day.

CHAPTER 9

Process and Release Exercise for Getting Into the Here and Now

Use the following exercise to help you release anyone or any situation from the past which is causing you any kind of emotional pain or distress. Daily use of this exercise provides an important way to free up energy and relieve mental stress, which will enable you to move more easily into the power of the present moment and remain there.

1. Identify all the people in your recent and distant past that have caused you distress. Next to his or her name, write a word or two that best describes the harm this person caused you.

2. Now, as you briefly reflect on each person in the list and the words you placed by each name, mentally place that person along with the harm they caused into an imaginary basket in front of you. While you do this for each person, speak or think the following words, "I AM fully and freely releasing ___ (individual's name) now, and I ask to be released in return for any pain that I have caused."

3. Next, pick up the imaginary basket that contains these people, events, and pain and hold this on your lap with your palms up. Take some time now to visualize yourself, every event, and individual that you placed into the basket engulfed in a blazing Violet Fire since this special energy and color will transmute everything it touches in amazing ways.

4. Now take some time to picture to yourself and the basket containing everyone and every event being flooded by a powerful waterfall of Divine white healing light which heals, cleanses, and renews everything it touches in tremendous ways.

5. Following this exercise and whenever you happen to think of any of these people or events again, simply remind yourself through the following God-power statement that this pain has been released and no longer holds any power to harm or upset you. I use statements like, "Thank you God for healing me and ___ individually and in our relationship as I AM completely cleansed in body, mind, and spirit of any negative memories and pain, which have been released into your hands and care."

6. You will always know if there is more release work to be done with a person or situation by using the following test. Think of a specific person or event, and if this still causes some type of emotional upset, there is still more release work to be done. This means to continue to focus on releasing and letting go of a particular person and/or situation daily until this is accomplished. Deeper hurts can often take more time to heal so keep working at this in order to gain the freedom you desire. Once you can think of the person, situation, and/or event without it impacting you negatively, then you will know that you are at the point where you can truly say that you have released and let go of something painful in your past.

7. Remember: Release work never means that the harm a person and/or event caused you was okay and acceptable. What it does mean is that choosing to forgive disempowers the poisons of anger and resentment so that they no longer negatively impact your body, mind, and spirit.

CH 9: Getting Into the Here and Now With Stillness – Part I

Set the timer for a particular period of time which can range anywhere from 5-20 minutes or longer. Sit in a comfortable position and begin to inhale deeply and pause for a moment before exhaling fully. Your eyes can be open or shut during this process. Continue to breathe deeply throughout the duration of this exercise and focus your attention on your breathing. Begin to notice what you are thinking about. If your mind is dwelling on thoughts from the past, open your eyes briefly if they are closed and place a check in the column marked "Past." When your mind moves to some future time or focus, open your eyes briefly if they are closed and place a check in the column marked "Future." You will know to place a check in the column marked "Present" when your thoughts have stopped and there is a deeper sense of peace and serenity within your mind. Notice how this feels because it is how you will feel when you enter into "the zone" experience, which was discussed throughout the accompanying chapter. Continue to keep track of your thoughts through the check marks you make. As you become more aware of your thoughts by stopping them when they move into the past or the future, you will notice that your mind will remain more and more in the present moment. Be sure to notice the additional energy you have in this state of mind and being. The goal of this exercise is to remain more and more in the present "now," since this is the only true moment that exists and one which is filled with an array of benefits and resources.

Past	Present	Future

CH 9: Getting Into the Here and Now With Stillness
(and without paperwork!) – Part II

1. Set the timer for a particular period of time which can range anywhere from 5-20 minutes or longer.

2. Sit in a comfortable position with one hand on top of each leg and begin to inhale deeply and pause for a moment before exhaling fully. Your eyes can be open or shut during this process.

3. Continue to breathe deeply throughout the duration of this exercise and focus your attention on your breathing.

4. Begin to notice what you are thinking about. If your mind is dwelling on thoughts from the past, tap your left leg with your left hand which represents thoughts from your "past." When your mind moves to some future time or focus, tap your right leg with your right hand which represents thoughts from your "future."

5. You will know you are in a "present" and "now" focus when your leg-tapping stops along with your thoughts, and there is a deeper sense of peace and serenity within your mind. Notice how this feels because it is how you will feel when you enter into "the zone" experience, which was discussed throughout the accompanying chapter.

6. Continue to take notice of your thoughts through tapping your different legs. As you become more aware of your thoughts by stopping them when they move into the past or the future, you will notice that your mind will remain more and more in the present moment.

7. Be sure to notice the additional energy you have in this state of mind and being.

8. The goal of this exercise is to remain more and more in the present "now," since this is the only true moment that exists and one which is filled with an array of benefits and resources.

CH 9: Using "The Wave" to Get Into the Present Moment – Part III

The following exercise is a very powerful one to use when disciplining your mind to stay in the present moment and under your control; consequently, I feel that this is an activity that should be accomplished at least twice per day.

1. Set the timer for a particular period of time which can range anywhere from 5-20 minutes or longer.

2. Sit or lie down in a comfortable position with one hand on each leg and begin to inhale deeply and pause for a moment before exhaling fully. Your eyes can be open or shut during this process, although I prefer to close my eyes whenever possible, so I can go within myself better.

3. Continue to breathe deeply throughout the duration of this exercise and as you do, picture a large wave of Divine light coming in and washing over you with every inhalation while every exhalation takes the wave along with your stress and any negativity back out to sea.

4. Stay completely in the present moment watching the large Divine wave of light come in with its renewing and restoring energy while cleansing you with each breath you exhale.

5. Begin to notice your thoughts whenever you stray from the present moment. If at any time your mind is dwelling on thoughts from the past, tap your left leg using your left hand which represents thoughts from your "past." If your mind happens to move to some future time or focus, tap your right leg using your right hand which represents thoughts from your "future."

6. You will know you are in a "present" and "now" focus when your leg-tapping stops along with your thoughts, and there is a deeper sense of peace and serenity within your mind. Notice how this feels because it is how you will feel when you enter into "the zone" experience, which was discussed throughout the accompanying chapter.

7. Continue to take notice of your thoughts through tapping your different legs. As you become more aware of your thoughts by stopping them when they move into the past or the future, you will notice that your mind will remain more and more in the present moment.

8. Be sure to notice the additional energy you have in this state of peaceful mind and being.

9. The goal of this exercise is to remain more and more in the present "now," since this is the only true moment that exists and one which is filled with an array of benefits and resources.

CH 9: Using a "No Thinking" Method for Getting Into the Here and Now – Part IV

1. The following method appears in the main book's chapter, "Overcoming the Adversary of Negative Thinking," but it needs to be included here as well because this technique rests on your ability to stay completely in the present moment.

2. As you focus totally and completely on your slower, deeper breathing, you also release any thoughts that come to mind by simply letting them go and giving them no additional attention. When you are exercising, waiting in line, or just sitting still, clear all of your thoughts from your mind and simply focus on your deeper breathing.

3. Focus on inhaling deeply for a few seconds, pausing for a couple of moments, exhaling for a few seconds, pausing for a couple of moments, and continuing in this pattern.

4. As you continue to focus on your deeper breathing, while staying completely in the present moment, keep erasing your mind from having any thoughts or thinking.

5. You can initially begin this by imagining and visualizing your mind as being a blank white writing board that has just been erased. When thoughts attempt to intrude, simply send them on their way by thinking "move along" and continue to focus on your deeper breathing with no thinking.

6. It takes practice to achieve this calm state of mind for any period of time. As you continue, notice how energizing and peaceful you feel because thinking often depletes us more than anything else. By controlling your thinking by not thinking, you conserve energy while re-energizing yourself too. In addition to teaching the mind how to stay fully and intensely focused on the present moment, this technique enables users to tap into "now" power.

7. When this technique is combined with stretching, biking, walking, or running, it enhances the activity because it gives us more energy for the activity since our thoughts and thinking are not draining us in any way.

8. Therefore, practice taking the time to discipline the mind to remain in that peaceful place which is found between our thoughts, because nowhere else will we find the power of the present moment equal to this elusive state of being.

CHAPTER 10
10 Steps to Visualizing and Creating Your Personal Desires (See pp. 110-124)

1). Describe in detail the goal or pursuit that you would like to create for yourself.

2). Spend time each day processing, releasing, and letting go of anyone or any situation that has caused you stress and resentment since this frees up energy needed to create.

3). Create a visualization schedule that you will use consistently until you achieve your goal.

7). List at least three things you will do daily to accomplish your desire and pursuit.

4). Visualization schedules involving more structured sessions answer questions like where and when this will occur, how often, and for how long. Always include brief and spontaneous visualization sessions too.

8). List at least three people who can support and help you in accomplishing your desire and pursuit. Be sure to describe what their specific assistance may include and involve.

Remember: Thoughts and Images
+
Feelings, Time, and Attention

Create

5). Create a 5-10 sentence statement or prayer that you will use prior to longer visualization sessions to seed your mind and help accomplish your pursuit.

9). List the positive (+) thoughts and feelings you experience whenever you think about your desire which is in the process of manifesting.

6). Create a one-sentence God-power statement or affirmation that will be used throughout the day to help you to connect to Source Energy, prevent negative thinking from negating your desire, and provide extra energy to accomplish your pursuit.

New Personal Life Experiences

10). List those that will celebrate the successful outcome and creation that you will soon experience. Be sure to note all of the unique ways that certain people will use to congratulate you.

CH 10: Visualizing to Improve Your Peak Performance – Part IA

1. Describe a specific area in which you would like to improve your performance. Include all the details of what you will visualize yourself experiencing, doing, and feeling while imagining a positive and desirable end result in the process. Use the next page if more space is needed.

2. Complete the personalized process and release chart or worksheet found in Part IC.

3-4). Visualization schedules ideally should include several 8-12 minute sessions especially upon waking and prior to sleep at night in addition to a session in between. Shorter visualizations can occur sporadically throughout the day.

Where will this occur? _____

When will this occur? _____

How often? _____

For how long? _____

5. Create a 5-10 sentence statement or prayer to use prior to longer visualization sessions that will help you to seed your mind and accomplish your pursuit. Use the next page if necessary.

CH 10: Visualizing to Improve Your Peak Performance
Part IA (continued)

CH 10: Visualizing to Improve Your Peak Performance – Part IB

6. Create a one-sentence affirmation/God-power statement that will be used throughout the day to help you to connect to Source Energy, prevent undesirable thinking from negating your desire, and accomplish your pursuit.

7. List some things you will do daily to accomplish this pursuit.

8. List the positive (+) thoughts and feelings you experience whenever you think about your desire which is in the process of manifesting.

9. List some people who can support you in accomplishing this pursuit and describe their help.

10. List the people who will celebrate the successful outcome and creation that you plan to experience. Then briefly note the unique ways that certain people will use to congratulate you.

CH 10: Personalized Process and Release Chart – Part IC

Write the initials of the person that needs to be processed and released.	List the primary event that is involved along with any thoughts about the situation.	List the primary feelings you experienced from this event.	List the things you will do to process and release the person and situation.	List what you have learned from the situation or event.	List what you have learned from the person involved.	Write an affirmation you will use to help release this person and event.	List your new perceptions of the person and the event after you have processed and released it.

Chapter 10 - Creating Through Visualization

CH 10: Personalized Process and Release Worksheet – Part IC

Write the initials of the person that needs to be processed and released.

List the primary event that is involved along with any thoughts about the situation.

List the primary feelings you experienced from this event.

List the things you will do to process and release the person and situation.

List what you have learned from the situation or event.

List what you have learned from the person involved.

Write an affirmation you will use to help release this person and event.

List your new perceptions of the person and the event after you have processed and released it.

CH 10: Visualizing to Improve Personal Healing – Part IIA

1. Describe a specific vision of the type of healing that you would like to experience. Include all the details of what you will visualize yourself experiencing, doing, and feeling while imagining a positive and desirable end result in the process. Use the next page if more space is needed.

2. Complete the personalized process and release chart or worksheet found in Part IIC.

3-4). Visualization schedules ideally should include several 8-12 minute sessions especially upon waking and prior to sleep at night in addition to a session in between. Shorter visualizations can occur sporadically throughout the day.

Where will this occur? _____

When will this occur? _____

How often? _____

For how long? _____

5. Create a 5-10 sentence statement or prayer to use prior to longer visualization sessions that will help you to seed your mind and accomplish your pursuit. Use the next page if necessary.

CH 10: Visualizing to Improve Personal Healing
Part IIA (continued)

CH 10: Visualizing to Improve Personal Healing – Part IIB

6. Create a one-sentence affirmation/God-power statement that will be used throughout the day to help you to connect to Source Energy, prevent undesirable thinking from negating your desire, and accomplish your pursuit.

7. List some things you will do daily to accomplish this pursuit.

8. List the positive (+) thoughts and feelings you experience whenever you think about your desire which is in the process of manifesting.

9. List some people who can support you in accomplishing this pursuit and describe their help.

10. List the people who will celebrate the successful outcome and creation that you plan to experience. Then briefly note the unique ways that certain people will use to congratulate you.

CH 10: Personalized Process and Release Chart – Part IIC

Write the initials of the person that needs to be processed and released.	List the primary event that is involved along with any thoughts about the situation.	List the primary feelings you experienced from this event.	List the things you will do to process and release the person and situation.	List what you have learned from the situation or event.	List what you have learned from the person involved.	Write an affirmation you will use to help release this person and event.	List your new perceptions of the person and the event after you have processed and released it.

CH 10: Personalized Process and Release Worksheet – Part IIC

Write the initials of the person that needs to be processed and released.

List the primary event that is involved along with any thoughts about the situation.

List the primary feelings you experienced from this event.

List the things you will do to process and release the person and situation.

List what you have learned from the situation or event.

List what you have learned from the person involved.

Write an affirmation you will use to help release this person and event.

List your new perceptions of the person and the event after you have processed and released it.

CH 10: Visualizing to Manifest Personal Desires – Part IIIA

1. Describe a specific desire that you would like to manifest. Include all the details of what you will visualize yourself experiencing, doing, and feeling while imagining a positive and desirable end result in the process. Use the next page if more space is needed.

2. Complete the personalized process and release chart or worksheet found in Part IIIC.

3-4). Visualization schedules ideally should include several 8-12 minute sessions especially upon waking and prior to sleep at night in addition to a session in between. Shorter visualizations can occur sporadically throughout the day.

Where will this occur? _____

When will this occur? _____

How often? _____

For how long? _____

5. Create a 5-10 sentence statement or prayer to use prior to longer visualization sessions that will help you to seed your mind and accomplish your pursuit. Use the next page if necessary.

CH 10: Visualizing to Manifest Personal Desires
Part IIIA (continued)

CH 10: Visualizing to Manifest Personal Desires – Part IIIB

6. Create a one-sentence affirmation/God-power statement that will be used throughout the day to help you to connect to Source Energy, prevent undesirable thinking from negating your desire, and accomplish your pursuit.

7. List some things you will do daily to accomplish this pursuit.

8. List the positive (+) thoughts and feelings you experience whenever you think about your desire which is in the process of manifesting.

9. List some people who can support you in accomplishing this pursuit and describe their help.

10. List the people who will celebrate the successful outcome and creation that you plan to experience. Then briefly note the unique ways that certain people will use to congratulate you.

CH 10: Personalized Process and Release Chart – Part IIIC

Write the initials of the person that needs to be processed and released.	List the primary event that is involved along with any thoughts about the situation.	List the primary feelings you experienced from this event.	List the things you will do to process and release the person and situation.	List what you have learned from the situation or event.	List what you have learned from the person involved.	Write an affirmation you will use to help release this person and event.	List your new perceptions of the person and the event after you have processed and released it.

Chapter 10 - Creating Through Visualization

CH 10: Personalized Process and Release Worksheet – Part IIIC

Write the initials of the person that needs to be processed and released.

List the primary event that is involved along with any thoughts about the situation.

List the primary feelings you experienced from this event.

List the things you will do to process and release the person and situation.

List what you have learned from the situation or event.

List what you have learned from the person involved.

Write an affirmation you will use to help release this person and event.

List your new perceptions of the person and the event after you have processed and released it.

CHAPTER 11
Avoiding Toxic Communication
Assertive Communication Self-Reflection Survey – PT I

1. Honest Communication

___ I am often completely honest and truthful in what I am saying to others (Yes/No). One exception to this relates to ___ (include a challenging person's initials here).

___ I am sometimes dishonest when speaking because I have a self-serving agenda. (Yes/No)

___ I am sometimes dishonest because it would be more hurtful than helpful. (Yes/No)

___ I am sometimes dishonest because it would have more of a negative than positive impact in the long run on others and/or myself. (Yes/No)

List the underlying reasons for your lack of honesty and specifically concerning ___ (include a challenging person's initials here).

2. Open / Direct Communication

___ I am often open and direct in all aspects of my communication. (Yes/No)

If you are concealing certain information, list what is preventing you from communicating this.

List what you need to address and what you are hesitant to say to someone.

3. Respectful Communication

___ I often speak in a manner which is kind and respectful. (Yes/No) If not…

List how you would feel if someone spoke to you in the manner that you are communicating.

List what you can do to improve this area of communication – especially with ___ (include a challenging person's initials here).

CH 11: Avoiding Toxic Communication
Assertive Communication Self-Reflection Survey – Part II

4. Congruent Speech / Behaviors

___ My words often match my actions, so I do what I say and say what I do. (Yes/No)

List the situations when you are likely to notice that your words do not match your actions.

List the people who are often nearby or involved when your words do not match your actions.

List the thoughts and feelings you experience when someone's words do not match their actions – especially when it concerns you.

List how your relationships were impacted whenever you noticed that someone's words did not match their actions – especially when it concerned you.

5. Empathy

___ I often put myself in another's shoes to see things from their point of view. (Yes/No)

___ I often take into consideration others' perspectives rather than just my own. (Yes/No)

List the times and situations that you have been more able to consider another's perspective.

___ I often take into consideration my needs rather than only pleasing others. (Yes/No)

List the ways you can begin to become more considerate of others' feelings and point of view.

List the ways you can begin to become more aware of your own needs, feelings, and point of view so this does not become suppressed and stressful.

CH 11: Avoiding Toxic Communication
Assertive Communication Self-Reflection Survey – Part III

Describe several different ways you use assertive communication, which is open, honest, direct, respectful, kind, and empathetic. Write what you say and how you say it.

List the people that receive this communication and describe how they might feel afterward.

Name_____ Describe resulting feelings_____

Name_____ Describe resulting feelings_____

Name_____ Describe resulting feelings_____

List the preferred methods you use to keep your assertive communication continuing.

Now write about a situation where assertive communication was very difficult to do. Write what you had to say, how you spoke your words, and what made this so difficult.

List any new thoughts, positive or spiritually-based affirmations, and/or feeling reminders that can help keep you focused on practicing assertive communication as opposed to using aggressive, passive, passive-aggressive, or victimology types of communication.

CH 11: Avoiding Toxic Communication Through the Use of "I" Statements – Part IV-a

Think about a stressful event that you would like to revisit using the following formula which can help you to communicate in a more open, honest, and direct manner.

I feel ___ when this situation involving _____ happens because _____.

1). **I feel** – List all the different ways you feel about this stressful event using the list below in combination with your own descriptive words that may fit better. Then choose 3-4 of the main feelings from your list that you were experiencing which can be plugged into this formula.

Exhausted	Overwhelmed	Embarrassed	Angry	Enraged
Confused	Hysterical	Happy	Ashamed	Hopeful
Ecstatic	Surprised	Frustrated	Mischievous	Cautious
Guilty	Bored	Lonely	Anxious	Sad
Suspicious	Disgusted	Superior	Hopeless	Shocked
Confident	Frightened	Depressed	Jealous	Shy
Helpless	Mad	Disappointed	Disturbed	Proud
Stupid	Tearful	Uncomfortable	Irritated	Betrayed
Loved	Sympathetic	Relieved	Foolish	Worried
Nervous	Insecure	Uncertain	Hurt	Annoyed
Inadequate	Determined	Satisfied	Worthless	Impressed
Trapped	Excited	Content	Motivated	Upset
Inspired	Unsafe	Bitter	Used	Abused
Understood	Lazy	Misunderstood	Trust	Mistrust
Unlovable	Pain	Misery	Rejected	Violated
Secure	Stable	Strong	Weakened	Defeated
_____	_____	_____	_____	_____

2). **When this situation involving ___ happens** – Now, write some details about the specific event, behavior, or situation that produces the feelings above.

CH 11: Avoiding Toxic Communication Through the Use of "I" Statements – Part IV-b

3). **Because** – Next, provide at least 3-4 different reasons that the specific event, behavior, or situation previously noted makes you feel a certain way.

4). Now, use the formula again to plug in the different elements from each of these specific areas so you will have several "I" statements to use for your assertive communication.

a). I feel _____

when this situation involving _____happens

because _____.

b). I feel _____

when this situation involving _____happens

because _____.

c). I feel _____

when this situation involving _____happens

because _____.

d). I feel _____

when this situation involving _____happens

because _____.

CH 11: Avoiding Toxic Communication – Aggressive Communication

Describe the ways you use aggressive communication (i.e., insults, bullying, making fun of others, speaking rudely). Write what you say and how you say it.

List the people that receive this communication and describe how they might feel afterward.

Name_____ Describe resulting feelings_____

Name_____ Describe resulting feelings_____

Name_____ Describe resulting feelings_____

List the methods you use to keep your aggressive communication continuing.

Now write what you can say to change your aggressive words to assertive communication which is open, direct, and respectful. Write what you can say, how you can say it, and what you will do differently.

List any new thoughts, positive or spiritually-based affirmations, and/or feeling reminders that can help keep you focused on practicing assertive communication as opposed to using aggressive types of communication.

CH 11: Avoiding Toxic Communication
Passive-Aggressive Communication

Describe the ways you use passive-aggressive communication (i.e., gossiping, speaking rudely about others without their knowing it, secretly using sabotaging words and/or behaviors). Write what you say and how you say it.

List the people that receive this communication and describe how they might feel afterward.

Name_____ Describe resulting feelings_____

Name_____ Describe resulting feelings_____

Name_____ Describe resulting feelings_____

List the methods you use to keep your passive-aggressive communication continuing.

Now write what you can say to change your passive-aggressive words to assertive communication which is open, direct, and respectful. Write what you can say, how you can say it, and what you will do differently.

List any new thoughts, positive or spiritually-based affirmations, and/or feeling reminders that can help keep you focused on practicing assertive communication as opposed to using passive-aggressive types of communication.

CH 11: Avoiding Toxic Communication – Passive Communication

Describe the ways you use passive communication or behaviors (i.e., to avoid expressing honest feelings and needs, to avoid confronting negative words or behaviors, allows oneself to be pushed around verbally and/or victimized). Write what you do not say or do.

List the people that receive this communication and describe how they might feel afterward.

Name_____ Describe resulting feelings_____

Name_____ Describe resulting feelings_____

Name_____ Describe resulting feelings_____

List the things you say and do to keep your passive communication continuing.

Now write what you can say or do to change your passive words and actions to assertive communication which is open, direct, and respectful. Write what you can say, how you can say it, and what you will do differently.

List any new thoughts, positive or spiritually-based affirmations, and/or feeling reminders that can help keep you focused on practicing assertive communication as opposed to using passive types of communication.

CH 11: Avoiding Toxic Communication – Victimology Communication

Describe the ways you use victim-like communication or behaviors (i.e., continuously talking about or dwelling on past hurts and wounds you have experienced, using your past as an excuse for not excelling or experiencing life, using your painful past experiences to manipulate others). Write what you say or do.

List the people that receive this communication and describe how they might feel afterward.

Name_____ Describe resulting feelings_____

Name_____ Describe resulting feelings_____

Name_____ Describe resulting feelings_____

List the things you say and do to keep your victimology communication continuing.

Now write what you can say or do to change your victim-like words and actions to assertive communication which is open, direct, and respectful. Write what you can say, how you can say it, and what you will do differently.

List any new thoughts, positive or spiritually-based affirmations, and/or feeling reminders that can help keep you focused on practicing assertive communication as opposed to using victimology types of communication.

CH 11: Resolving Difficult Relationships/Situations – Part I

1). Make a list of the people you need to release from anger, resentments, negative feelings, and communication patterns.

2). For each person, write, think, or imagine speaking to that person (living or deceased) in the following way:

a). I appreciate from you… (Describe what you appreciated from your relationship with this person because there are always positive and negative sides to everyone.)

b). I was hurt by… (Describe the things that hurt you from your relationship with this person.)

c). I am sorry for… (Describe the things that you did to hurt this person and your relationship.)

d). I needed more…from you. (Describe all the things that you needed more of in your relationship with this person.)

CH 11: Resolving Difficult Relationships/Situations – Part II

e). I miss these things about you and our relationship including… (Describe what you miss.)

f). I didn't get to tell you that… (Describe what you did not get to say to the person.)

g). I am now choosing to release all pain, hurt, and stress relating to… (Describe the event and what you plan to do to release it.)

h). I learned___ from this person and situation. (Describe all the things that you learned from your relationship with this person.)

Take as much time as you need with each person before moving to the next person on the list. You decide the number of people on your list that you will process before you proceed to the next step of the exercise, which involves release.

CH 11: Resolving Difficult Relationships/Situations – Part III

3). Next, slowly speak a statement like the one below to "let go," cleanse, and release all negative events, stressors, people, communication patterns, and memories, which can act as poisons to our body, mind, and spirit. Use the longer passage below in a relaxed state of mind for 5-10 minutes in the morning, afternoon, evening, and especially right before going to sleep since the deeper, powerful "being" aspect of the self is very open to suggestion when it is relaxed.

I am fully and freely letting go and releasing everyone and every situation that has ever caused me stress, anger, pain, or discomfort, and this includes ___. Thank you God I am now being released from everyone and any situation that I have ever caused stress, anger, discomfort, or pain to, and this includes ___. Thank you I am being cleansed inside and out of all negative thoughts, words, memories, pain, and behaviors of all kinds that are buried deep within me. Thank you for cutting all the cords and attachments which link me to hurtful thoughts, events, people, and memories within. I know and believe I can do all things and overcome any problems through the God power within which strengthens me. Thank you God I AM being cleansed, healed, and strengthened in body, mind, and spirit as every cell, organ, and tissue is restored by day and by night to greater peace, harmony, health, healing, and wholeness.

4). Now see yourself with divine help putting all the negativity you are releasing into large plastic trash bags that are carried outside of your house (or self) and placed into an incinerating dumpster. As you return to your house, picture yourself along with those you have just released standing in a circle with one or more spiritual masters (i.e., Buddha, Moses, Mohammed, Jesus, a saint, angel, prophet, ascended master or holy one, etc.) under a celestial waterfall which fills everyone's body, mind, and spirit with healing and renewing Divine white light.

5). Next, imagine and feel the uplifting emotions and feelings you will experience from letting go and releasing all negativity which is replaced with Divine healing light, peace, and restoration. Doing these exercises consistently will connect you with Source Energy while reprograming your deeper mind and self to go about making your release and resolution happen.

6). Anytime you experience any negative feelings in between the times you are using the longer exercise above, use a shorter "tune-in" like the ones below, which are brief and powerful affirmations, that will continue to help you heal by releasing negativity and changing your mindset. Using a God-power statement below or one of your making for several minutes by thinking or speaking these enriching words slowly will change your negative thinking and feelings and replace them with peaceful thoughts and emotions. Repeat as often as necessary.

Thank you God for your Divine restoration and perfect work healing me individually and in my relationship with ___ (person's initials), so that all negative communication patterns and memories are released and resolved to the highest good of everyone involved.

Thank you God I AM being healed and cleansed individually and in my relationship with ___ (person's initials), so that all negative communication patterns and memories are released and resolved to the highest good of everyone involved.

CHAPTER 12

Reflection Checklist for Developing New Friendships – Part I

The following questions will help you think about different issues related to developing new friendships. Careful reflection on these questions will help you to understand past and present attitudes toward developing friendships as well as different ways to go about this in the future.

1. How many new friendships have you made recently?

2. How and where did you meet these people?

> ** *Think about why this is – or is not happening – in your life.*

3. What interests did you have in common?

4. Are you friendly toward others you do not know well or at all? **

5. Do you first have to be introduced before you will talk to someone you do not know? **

6. Do you greet and smile at others only if they are the opposite or same sex? **

7. Do you make an effort to talk with others you do not know well or at all? **

8. Do you ask others questions in an effort to find out more about them? **

9. Do you spend time talking about and focusing only on your interests and pursuits? **

10. Do you speak to others you do not know only when you need something from them? **

11. Do you speak to others you know only when you want or need something from them? **

12. Do you limit your conversations to only those you know or have known for a while? **

13. Do you want to make new friendships with those outside your circle of friends and family?

14. Have you tried making new friends with those outside your circle of friends and family? **

15. What makes you hesitant about meeting new people?

16. How much time do you have available for meeting new people?

17. Where are the most likely places for you to meet new people?

18. What activities are most likely to bring you in contact with new potential friends?

19. When looking to make new friends, think about how important is the person's age, race, sex, income, education, beliefs, sexual orientation, and ethnicity.

20. On a scale of 1 – 10 with 10 being the strongest "yes" and 1 being an absolute "no," how open are you to developing new friendships at this time?

CH 12: Reflections to Have Better Relationships – Part II

1. Take a moment to reflect upon whether you are being kind and respectful to everyone you know and interact with on a consistent basis. Write the initials of those that you feel you can improve your level of kindness, communication, and/or behavior toward.

2. Because thinking initiates the process of making changes within ourselves, write some ways that you can begin to think differently about some of these people noted above.

3. Write some ways that you can speak differently to and about some of these people.

4. Write some ways that you can act differently to improve relationships with certain people.

5. Write the spiritual practices that you will use to help resolve issues with certain people.

6. Write down the people that can assist you in strengthening your relationships and briefly describe how they can help.

CH 12: Formulating the Practice of "Letting Go" and Releasing Others – Part I-a

One way to take back your power and remove any mental-emotional poisons from within is by making a list of all the people and situations from your past that have been hurtful and need to be released. This list can include parents, family members and relatives, current and former partners, friends, teammates, co-workers, bosses, teachers, coaches, and virtually anyone that has caused you pain or harm. Begin by thinking back to your earliest memories of your family and grade school; then reflect year by year to see if any memories with others stand out as being harmful and in need of being released and let go. Make a list using people's initials now.

After making your list, use the script below as a guide to assist you in the release process. Feel free to use any part of the formula and include your own ideas as well. You may think, speak, or write out your release work in a paragraph because the most important thing is to simply do it. It is also important to know that when letting go and releasing others, forgiveness does not mean that someone's harmful words or actions were okay. Instead, it means that although the harm you experienced will never be acceptable, you have chosen not to hold this anger any longer since this gives the person and the situation power over you. Releasing and letting go of harmful emotions also cleanses the holistic self of toxins and all the accompanying negativity related to a painful event. Some hurtful events and people may require numerous release sessions, so feel free to use this example as often as you need to in order to let go of any negative memories. You will know when you are close to finishing your release work because thinking about the person and the event will not be emotionally hurtful for you anymore.

From your list of people above, use the following script to think, speak, or write about each person and the event using any or all parts of the following sentences in addition to any extra information you may choose to include. Use the next page for your written processing work.

I feel ____ (describe all the ways you feel) because of the situation involving ____. This situation is upsetting and ____ (describe feelings) for me especially because ____. I appreciate that ____. I was hurt by ____. I needed more ____. This person and/or situation taught me ____.

I choose to let go and release ____ (write the person's initials) and the situation involving ____ because it will help heal me while releasing the negative memory of the event and everyone involved. I also ask to be released and forgiven from those I have harmed especially involving ____ so we can all move on to experiencing greater healing, peace, and harmony in the future.

I apologize for my role in this situation involving ____ because ____. I am sorry for my role in hurting ____ and ____ during this situation because of what I said ____ (note what you said) and did ____ (note what you did). My hope for ____ (person's initials) and the situation is that ____.

After you have thought, spoken, or written about a hurtful event, the practice of "letting go" and releasing a person and any negative feelings is often strengthened by tearing up and/or burning the paragraph you wrote which helps to solidify your release. Then, imagine shaking hands or hugging the person you wish to release in the presence of a Divine mediator since this will enable a peaceful resolution. Afterward, refuse to think or speak about the situation since it was "let go" unless you are in the process of performing another release session.

CH 12: "Letting Go" and Releasing Through Written Processing – Part I-b

I feel _____ (describe

all the ways you feel) because of the situation involving _____.

This situation is upsetting and _____ (describe

feelings) for me especially because _____

_____.

I appreciate that _____.

I was hurt by _____.

I needed more _____.

This person and/or situation taught me _____.

I choose to let go and release _____ (write the person's initials) and the situation involving

_____

because it will help heal me while releasing the negative memory of the event and everyone involved.

I also ask to be released and forgiven from those I have harmed especially involving _____

_____ so we can

all move on to experiencing greater healing, peace, and harmony in the future. I apologize for my

role in this situation involving _____ because

_____

_____.

I am sorry for my role in hurting _____ and _____

during this situation because of what I said _____

(note what you said) and did _____

(note what you did). My hope for _____ (person's initials) and the situation is that _____

_____

_____.

CH 12: Releasing Others Through Conversation With a Trustworthy Friend – Part II

1. Take 10-20 minutes to describe a negative event that you experienced with a trustworthy friend. List some points that you will discuss.

2. Talk about the different people involved in the situation and describe what hurt you most. List some points that you will discuss.

3. Discuss your feelings about "letting go" and releasing the people involved in this situation. List some points that you will discuss.

4. Describe your role in this situation and how you may have unintentionally added to your personal pain and hurt. List some points that you will discuss.

5. Describe how you may have hurt others that were involved in the situation; be sure to include forgiving yourself in the process. List some points that you will discuss.

6. Indicate your present motivation level for wanting to "let go" and release this person, the situation, and yourself too.

1   2   3   4   5   6   7   8   9   10

Very little   Moderately   Very much

7. Personal Contract. Read and then sign this brief contract in the presence of the trustworthy friend you are speaking to in order to solidify your commitment to this process of release.

I _____ (write your signature) vow to sincerely work on letting go and releasing _____ _____ (list each person's initials) and the situation involving _____ so that we can all move on from this negative event to experience greater peace, harmony, healing, and resolution.

Date_____ Time _____

CH 12: Using Truce Cards to "Let Go" and Release Others – Part III

1. Create an affirmation and/or God-power statement that will continue to assist you in "letting go" of any negative event and those involved. Example: "Thank you God for Divine healing, peace, and resolution between ___ and myself to the highest good of everyone involved."

2. Whenever you feel the need to contact an individual that you have just "let go" and released, you may choose to speak in person or by phone, send a letter or an email, or simply give the person a copy of the Truce Card below to symbolize a peaceful ending and resolution to the situation. Do not hesitate to write a letter or speak directly to someone who is deceased since this will enable you to convey your message and let go of the person at the same time.

Using and/or Creating a Truce Card That Fits You Best

This Truce Card is my promise to make peace (a truce) with this card's receiver, and I am "letting go" of any negative thoughts, words, behaviors, and feelings I am holding. My hope is that the recipient will do the same in return.	This Truce Card is my promise
This Truce Card means I _____ _____ promise to make peace (a truce) with this card's receiver, and I am "letting go" of any negative thoughts, words, behaviors, and feelings I am holding. My hope is that the recipient will do the same in return.	This Truce Card means

3. Once you have performed all of these steps, know that you are well on your way to "letting go" and releasing any person and/or negative event from your life. You may feel the need to repeat the previous steps by discussing the same person and situation with up to several trustworthy friends at some point in the future. It is helpful that any time you process a negative or hurtful situation by writing and/or talking about it that this is always followed by a release and "letting go" of the situation. Writing and/or talking about hurtful events from the past that do not include a release of the situation afterward can keep someone stuck in a victimology mindset that keeps replaying a painful situation without focusing on healing, releasing hurtful feelings and people permanently, so that you can finally move on. If you feel more release work is still necessary, using part IV of these releasing exercises, which is found on the next page, is a very powerful method to ensure completion of this task.

CH 12: "Letting Go" and Releasing Others Through Focused Time-Outs – Part IV

The following exercise is a very powerful and effective way to practice "letting go" in order to cleanse and release hurtful events, people, and poisons that you have accumulated and may still remain within your soul, body, mind, and spirit. Therefore, slowly read a passage like the one below silently or out loud for 5-10 minutes several times each day for at least 21 days and especially just before going to sleep since your deeper mind and powerful "being" self are very relaxed and open to suggestion which enable your release and resolution to happen.

> *Thank you God I AM fully and freely letting go and releasing everyone and every situation that has ever caused me stress, anger, pain, or discomfort in any way. This particularly includes ___ and involves ___. I also ask to be released from everyone and any situation that I have ever caused stress, anger, discomfort, or pain to in any way. This particularly includes ___ and involves ___. Thank you I am being vacuumed and cleansed inside and out of all negative thoughts, words, memories, pain, and actions of all kinds which are buried deep within. Thank you for your Divine restoration's perfect work cutting all the cords and attachments which link me to negative thoughts, events, people, and memories. I now imagine myself with Divine help bagging up all the negativity I am releasing by putting it into large trash bags and carrying all this debris outside of my house (or self) so I can place it into the garbage dumpster. Thank you I AM being cleansed and healed in soul, body, mind, and spirit as every cell, organ, and tissue is restored tremendously by day and by night to greater peace, health, and well-being. Thank you I AM being completely cleansed and healed from all painful memories which are replaced with Divine light, resolution, peace, and forgiveness in God's name.*

After slowing repeating these words and imagining your cleansing taking place within, see yourself sitting under a Divine waterfall which refills your soul, body, mind, and spirit with healing white light. Then, be sure to feel and sense all the grateful feelings you will experience while you become healed, re-energized, and restored because this will prompt your deeper mind and "being" self to go about making it happen. Essentially, this means that you imagine and actually feel the joy and thrill of a friend coming up to you and then hugging or shaking your hand as he or she tells you how much more centered and at peace you seem to be now. You will always know when you are close to finishing your release work with any individual or incident because thinking about the person and the event will not be hurtful for you anymore. Be sure to repeat this process as often as needed.

CH 12: Trust vs. Mistrust

Trust is an essential foundation for relationships of all kinds, and yet, most people have had their trust broken in some way. Complete the following worksheet to better understand your own experiences involving trust. Then with a close friend, discuss some ways that people, including yourself, can become more trusting as well as trustworthy in their relationships.

Describe a situation where you have had trust broken in a close relationship.

Describe any thoughts and feelings that accompanied this situation.

How did this affect your ability to trust others after this situation?

Did you ever fully regain trust with this person again? Explain.

Explain some ways that you can become more trusting of others despite your experience.

Explain some ways that you can become a more trustworthy individual in your own relationships.

CH 12: Becoming a Leader While Avoiding the "Sheep Syndrome"

Briefly describe an instance where you avoided confronting someone with honest thoughts, words, actions, and feelings because you felt pressure not to confront or address a problem.

Write what you needed to think about differently during this situation.

Write what you needed to say differently during this situation.

Write what you needed to do differently during this situation.

List any feelings such as fear that kept you from addressing a person or situation in the way that you felt you should have done.

Rate how scary those feelings are now? (Smaller)   1   2   3   4   5   (Larger)

Write an affirmation or God-power statement to remind you of the powerlessness of fear when you remember to connect to the supreme power of your Source.

Who will support you when you address future difficulties and note how they will do this?

Write what you will think, say, and do differently the next time you encounter a similar event.

CH 12: Overcoming Personal Disengagement and Detachment

Characteristics that suggest personal disengagement (Y = Yes / N = No / U = Unsure)

___ I dislike bonding and/or communicating with others or specific others in deeper ways.
___ I keep a more detached and distant attitude toward others, including specific others.
___ I keep an attitude that another's life and issues are not usually my business or concern.
___ I often think, speak, and act in ways that create distance and separateness from others.
___ I am willing to closely examine and even change the way I create distance with others.

List some specific attitudes you can release that will promote greater bonding with others.

List some things you can do to allow yourself to bond more readily with others.

List some ways you can speak that will allow yourself to bond more readily with others.

List the spiritual practices that will enhance your ability to better bond with others.

List some people's initials that you are willing to begin using these better bonding techniques with.

List the people that can help you to better bond with others and note how they can help.

CH 12: Overcoming Personal Enmeshment and Entanglement

Characteristics that suggest personal enmeshment (Y = Yes / N = No / U = Unsure)

____ I have an excessive need to bond, communicate, or socialize with others or specific others.
____ I have an excessive need to know details about someone's personal life on a constant basis.
____ I have an attitude that a friend's life and affairs are essentially my life and business as well.
____ I act and speak in ways which often promote unhealthy bonding/entanglements with others.
____ I am willing to examine and even change the way I create unhealthy bonds with others.

List some specific attitudes you can release that will promote healthy individuality, independence, and separateness from others.

List some things you can do to experience a more separate and independent lifestyle.

List some ways to speak that will prevent you from becoming overly involved in others' lives.

List the spiritual practices that will enhance your ability to be more of an independent person.

List the people's initials that you are willing to begin giving more space to.

List the people that can help you become more of an independent person and briefly note how they can help.

CHAPTER 13
Checklist of Desirable Traits in Partners... and Oneself – Part I

The following checklist will help you to examine yourself as well as prospective partners' characteristics in order to help you decide if someone has potential for a deeper relationship. Having at least 7 out of 11 checkmarks in each area is most desirable for prospective partners as long as you have similar numbers too. When doing this exercise, be extremely honest in your evaluations and expectations. Look closely at potential partners that lack initiative in any of the areas below since this often becomes an issue over time. Remember that for "soulmate" relationships, the spiritual self, which includes consistent spiritual practices, is most important.

Actively working on the Spiritual Self may include:

___ Belief in a Higher Benevolent Power that includes action steps which promote a growing relationship with your Source.

___ Spends ample time in prayer, contemplation, and/or meditation daily.

___ Feeds their spirit with inspirational and/or spiritual material daily.

___ Values teachings that promote loving God and goodness and others like our self.

___ Values spiritual growth and learning from teachers, ministers, rabbis, priests, and/or self-study as well as fellowship with others.

___ Refuses to judge, criticize, and/or condemn those who are different.

___ Allows others to grow spiritually in ways that differ from their own beliefs and practices.

___ Values assisting others in need who are not only family and friends.

___ Displays uplifting traits such as acceptance, forgiveness, compassion, patience, tolerance, humility, kindness, and honesty in thought, words, and actions consistently in daily life.

___ Holds similar interests, beliefs, and "doing" behaviors regarding spirituality as you do.

___ Specify any personal requirement(s) pertaining to spiritual interests and/or pursuits.

Actively working on the Mental, Emotional, and Energetic Self may include:

___ Engages in life-long learning while valuing and encouraging this in others.

___ Ability to notice problems in the making and take intelligent steps to avoid escalating troubles.

___ Ability to overcome unforeseen difficulties through problem solving and/or conflict resolution.

CH 13: Checklist of Desirable Traits in Partners… and Oneself – Part II

___ Holds an idealistic view of the world and people (i.e., everyone deserves to be treated fairly and kindly regardless of their race, ethnicity, gender, religion, sexual orientation, disability, beliefs, lifestyle, etc.).

___ Holds a similar view of personal values (i.e., what you think is important) such as being a hard worker, good parent, kind and honest person, and someone who goes out of their way to help others – or not).

___ Positive, optimistic thinker (i.e., sees a glass as half full and not half empty, sees the good in others more so than the bad).

___ Demonstrates control over their thinking and emotions rather than allowing negative feelings and mindsets such as anger, resentment, sadness, disappointment, regret, fear, anxiety, guilt, and shame to control them.

___ Ability to manage stress well; does not remain down or depressed for long.

___ Displays higher energy and good "vibes" by generally being an uplifting person to be around.

___ Values and enjoys their chosen life path which can include a certain career, parenting, special work, interests, and/or hobbies.

___ Specify any personal requirement(s) pertaining to the mental, emotional, and energetic self.

Actively working on the Relational Self may include:

___ Ability to effectively resolve disagreements and/or conflict with others, including intimate partners.

___ Ability to effectively listen, share, and negotiate with others, including intimate partners.

___ Ability to effectively resolve unfinished issues within the self that stem from past problems with caretakers, family members, friendships, and/or partnerships, since this can carry into the present and impact current relationships.

___ Values learning new ways to better friendships and intimate relationships.

___ Displays open, honest communication consistently and is able to speak from the heart.

___ Has uplifting people in their life and chooses the company they keep wisely.

CH 13: Checklist of Desirable Traits in Partners... and Oneself – Part III

___ Viewed as a positive influence to be around with an ability to laugh and make light of situations; avoids engaging in excessive negative communication patterns.

___ Knows how to get along and compromise with others; enjoys interacting with others.

___ Ability to release negative thoughts and feelings such as anger and resentments in order to avoid poisoning oneself and his or her personal relationships.

___ Displays authentic speech and behavior that match because you do what you say and say what you do; places a high value on being honest, faithful, and trustworthy.

___ Specify any personal requirement(s) pertaining to the relational self.

Actively working on the Physical Self by:

___ Strengthens the physical self consistently through daily healthy eating habits, engaging in strength training, aerobic activities, flexibility work, and other types of exercise.

___ Supports the physical self consistently through proper rest, sleep, medical and dental care.

___ Develops the physical self consistently through the use of uplifting words and actions that include life-enhancing practices such as volunteering and/or random acts of kindness.

___ Avoids addictive habits and unhealthy behaviors of all kinds including work-a-holism, gambling, excessive and/or compulsive use of technology, tobacco, alcohol, and/or drugs.

___ Displays competence in living a healthy lifestyle that avoids reckless and/or risk-taking behavior, which may involve ethically questionable and/or dishonest practices of all kinds.

___ Displays competence in their employment through healthy attitudes and consistent work performance.

___ Displays competence in money management, avoids overspending, and excessive debt.

___ Avoids overly materialistic mindsets that prioritize acquiring wealth and physical possessions over other aspects of the holistic self in addition to others' well-being.

___ Strives to consistently maintain higher levels of self-care and attractiveness through healthy living practices that also uplift others through helpful gestures, words, and deeds.

___ Holds similar interests, beliefs, and "doing" behaviors regarding physical well-being.

___ Specify any personal requirement(s) pertaining to the physical self.

CH 13: Polishing the Soul and Self to Experience a Soulmate Relationship – Part I

Describe what you are doing to improve each of the different areas of the self in order to become a soulmate and have the special relationship you desire. Remember: A soulmate is – only – as a soulmate does, speaks, and thinks; plus, if you desire a soulmate, you must work on becoming one too.

I am actively working on my spiritual self by: (How often? How long? When is this done?)

I am actively working on my mental self by: (How often? How long? When is this done?)

I am actively working on my emotional self by: (How often? How long? When is this done?)

CH 13: Polishing the Soul and Self to Experience a Soulmate Relationship – Part II

Describe what you are doing to improve each of the different areas of the self in order to become a soulmate and have the special relationship you desire. Remember: A soulmate is – only – as a soulmate does, speaks, and thinks; plus, if you desire a soulmate, you must work on becoming one too.

I am actively working on my energetic self by: (How often? How long? When is this done?)

I am actively working on my relational self by: (How often? How long? When is this done?)

I am actively working on my physical self by: (How often? How long? When is this done?)

CH 13: Polishing the Soul and Self to Experience a Soulmate Relationship – Part III

Now, write several affirmations and/or God-power statements that will help you transform your current relationship into the special partnership you desire. While these should be performed individually each day, they become even more powerful when they are said consistently with your partner. (Sample: Thank you God for blessing, healing and helping ___ and myself individually and in our relationship by filling our partnership with greater love, commitment, peace, harmony, joy, communication, compatibility, respect, kindness, and forgiveness.)

CH 13: Polishing the Soul and Self to Experience a Soulmate Relationship – Part IV

Apology Letter

Dear _____, I _____ am very sorry for any stress, pain, and harm that I have caused you during our relationship in the past. I apologize for my mistakes, and I _____ am asking for your forgiveness. Some of the things I am most sorry for are on my list below. (You can use another sheet of paper if necessary.)

Please list any other mistakes that were hurtful and were not included on my list.

While I cannot go back and undo my mistakes, I _____ really want to correct my mistakes by trying each day, one day at a time, to do my best with you and in our relationship. I want to begin this work on (Date _____). I will also continue to work on improving our relationship by doing the following steps below.

I _____ am also offering my forgiveness to you for the times I have been hurt by you in our relationship. I am offering my forgiveness so I can let go of my hurt pertaining to the following situations on my list below. (You can use another sheet of paper if necessary.)

Again, I _____ am sorry for my mistakes and ask your forgiveness. I promise to forgive you for the times I have been hurt as well. I _____ believe if we can both forgive and be forgiven that this will help to strengthen our relationship and move it forward. I _____ also promise to continue to work on our relationship, forgive you, and ask to be forgiven whenever we make mistakes in the future since we both know this will happen.

Signature of Letter Writer _____ Date_____

I, Signature of Partner, _____ Date_____
accept your apology, forgive you as well, and promise to do my part to better our partnership.

CH 13: Polishing the Soul and Self to Experience a Soulmate Relationship – Part V

Weekly Acts of Kindness List - Provide your partner with a list of kindly acts that s/he could do for you each week to make your days more pleasant. Next, make a list of things to do together at various times as well as places you can go. These activities are performed with an attitude of love and with your partner's well-being in mind. Be sure you perform all acts of good will with no expectations of returned favors and with no strings attached.

Kindly Acts That Will Make My Day More Pleasant.

Partner #1 List   Partner #2 List

Things We Can Do Together

Partner #1 List   Partner #2 List

Places We Can Go Together

Partner #1 List   Partner #2 List

CH 13: Goal-Setting to Experience a Soulmate Relationship
Part VI-a
(Part VI-a-c is adapted from the ideas of Elaine Wetzel)

Use this worksheet to help you and your partner identify some new goals for the next year that will help to improve your relationship and your individual selves too.

1). Improving the Physical Self and Health – This can include implementing new activities such as healthier eating, regular exercise, different leisure interests, joining a health-oriented group or club, and replacing unhealthy physical habits with new life-enhancing practices.

Goal(s):

Describe the steps that you and your partner will take to achieve these goals in the next year.

2). Improving the Mental and Intellectual Self – This can include implementing new learning activities such as reading, artwork, choir, musical instruments, and attending new educational opportunities that include classes, workshops, clubs, discussion or interest groups, and lectures.

Goal(s):

Describe the steps that you and your partner will take to achieve these goals in the next year.

CH 13: Goal-Setting to Experience a Soulmate Relationship
Part VI-b

Use this worksheet to help you and your partner identify some new goals for the next year that will help to improve your relationship and your individual selves too.

3). Improving the Energetic and Emotional Self – This can include implementing new activities such as mindfulness, meditation, fun-time events, yoga or flexibility programs, learning new stress reduction methods, monitoring negative thinking, and replacing unhealthy stress-producing habits with positive coping practices.

Goal(s):

Describe the steps that you and your partner will take to achieve these goals in the next year.

4). Improving the Soul and Spiritual Self – This can include implementing new activities such as inspirational reading, prayer and meditation, group study or worship, practicing random and/or calculated acts of kindness, attending spiritually based classes, workshops, lectures, healing, or discussion groups.

Goal(s):

Describe the steps that you and your partner will take to achieve these goals in the next year.

CH 13: Goal-Setting to Experience a Soulmate Relationship
Part VI-c

Use this worksheet to help you and your partner identify some new goals for the next year that will help to improve your relationship and your individual selves too.

3). Improving the Relational Self and Your Relationship – This can include implementing new activities such as daily talk time, hand-feet-neck massages, fun activities and dates, including day trips, couples getaways, retreats, workshops, or counseling, and identifying unhealthy relational habits and replacing them with positive uplifting practices.

Goal(s):

Describe the steps that you and your partner will take to achieve these goals in the next year.

4). Improving the Miscellaneous – This can include implementing new practices such as better financial management with accompanying goals, home improvement or landscaping projects, and improving the division of labor and chores that occur within the home.

Goal(s):

Describe the steps that you and your partner will take to achieve these goals in the next year.

CH 13: Polishing the Soul and Self to Experience a Soulmate Relationship – Part VII

Burying Treasures Into Your Partner's Restful Mind
(Adapted from the ideas of Peter Woodbury)

The following exercise is a very powerful and effective way to seed your partner's soul, body, mind, and spirit with an array of treasures which so few people get to hear and experience. In the 7-10 minutes just before your partner is beginning to fall asleep, gently tell them as many uplifting things regarding the qualities you admire most about them, their work, the successes you hope to see them accomplish, and anything else you can think of that the person would like to hear. The beauty and power of this exercise lies in the fact that just before going to sleep, the deeper mind and powerful "being" self are very relaxed and open to suggestion which will enable your uplifting words to take root and manifest more readily in this person's life. Alternate each night between giving and receiving verbal treasures with your partner.

The following is an example of one such script you can use although it is best to personalize this information with your own words which relate specifically to your special partner.

> *You are a special, loving, and amazing child of the Divine that I am grateful to have as my loving partner. I appreciate all that you are, all that you do, and especially your special qualities including ___. Our love and relationship grows stronger day by day as our family is blessed and prospered in all ways. You are accomplishing all the wonderful things that you have chosen to do, and your talents and gifts are blessing more people everywhere. As a child of the Divine, you are thriving in all you do and whatever you need to accomplish your goals and unique work will flow easily and peacefully to you. You are blessed in all ways as the hand of the Lord is upon you and everything you touch. Your kind and loving presence blesses everyone you meet. Only good things happen to you as you are being blessed more and more every day in every way. You are protected, healed, awakened, and restored every day in every way. You are fulfilling the purposes of God's plan for your life each and every day. (Repeat this several times)*

Now, take some time to think about and/or ask your partner to provide you with some ideas, words, and statements that he or she would like to listen to since this will strengthen and enhance the words you are seeding in his or her mind. List any additional points below that you can tell your partner as he or she drifts off to sleep.

Then, so you and/or your partner do not negate any of these desires, think and speak throughout the day an affirmation or God-power statement such as, "Thank you God I AM being blessed, prospered, and ___ all day in every way" which is positive thinking at its best while connecting people to their Source in ways that will open doors in life that would not be accessible otherwise. Write your special affirmation or God-power statement below.

CH 13: Burying Treasures Into Your Child's Restful Mind – Part VIII
(Adapted from the ideas of Peter Woodbury)

The following exercise is a very powerful and effective way to seed your child's soul, body, mind, and spirit with an array of treasures which so few people get to hear and experience. In the 7-10 minutes just before your child is beginning to fall asleep, gently tell him or her as many uplifting things about the qualities you admire most about them, the successes you hope to see them accomplish, and anything else you can think of that a child would like to hear. The beauty and power of this exercise lies in the fact that just before going to sleep, the deeper mind and powerful "being" self are very relaxed and open to suggestion which will enable your uplifting words to take root and manifest more readily in this child's life.

The following is an example of one such script you can use although it is best to personalize this information with your own words which relate specifically to your special child.

> *You are a special, loving and kind child who will accomplish all the wonderful things that you have come to bless the Earth with. You will be successful and share all the excellent talents and gifts that you have within you with all the people you will meet. You are an amazing child of the Divine that will thrive in everything you do. Whatever you need to accomplish your goals and unique work will flow easily and peacefully to you because you are blessed in all ways and will be throughout your entire life. You are kind, loving, and bless everyone that you meet. Only good things happen to you as you are blessed in all ways more and more every day. You are becoming more healthy, loving, kind, intelligent, strong, healed, and whole every day in every way. You are fulfilling the purposes of God's plan for your life each and every day. (Repeat this several times)*

Now, take some time to think about and/or ask your child to provide you with some ideas, words, and statements that he or she would like to listen to since this will strengthen and enhance the words you are seeding in his or her mind. List any additional points below that you can tell your child as he or she drifts off to sleep.

Then, so you and/or your child do not negate any of these desires, think and speak throughout the day an affirmation or God-power statement such as, "Thank you God I AM (or insert a child's name here ___ is) being blessed, protected, healed, and ___ every day in every way" which is positive thinking at its best while connecting people to their Source in ways that will open doors in life that would not be accessible otherwise. Write your special affirmation or God-power statement below.

CH 13: Using Spiritual Resources to Attract Your Special Partner
Part IX

Use the following steps to help attract your special partner.

1). Raise your consciousness and spiritualize this daily by connecting often to your Source so that you become the type of partner you wish to attract. Cultivating traits such as honesty, loyalty, and kindness are, in fact, spiritual qualities rather than human characteristics, which suggests that these can always be improved upon.

2). Write out in detail below what you desire in a partner and spend time each day picturing what your life would be like with this person while you are in a more relaxed state of mind.

3). Then, begin thinking and speaking an affirmation such as, "Thank you I AM being connected to my divinely appointed partner in God's perfect way and time." Be sure to imagine and try to experience how you will feel when this comes to pass by visualizing the joyful outcome which might include people congratulating you at some special event.

4). Know and believe that this will come to pass in divine order when you are most ready to receive your special relationship. Also realize that any current relationship that is not part of your divine plan must transform or end in order for you to experience a soulful relationship.

5). Remain open to meeting new people since you never know how or when you will meet this special person.

Describe in detail your ideal partner's characteristics.

Describe in detail your life in an uplifting and soulful partnership.

CHAPTER 14
Emotions: Your Special Guide and Rudder – Part I

Briefly describe a situation where you *knew* you were **out of balance** by the feelings you were experiencing. What were you doing, saying, or thinking that made you know something was wrong?

Describe all the feelings that you had relating to this situation and how you *knew* they were a warning.

List any thoughts that you remember having during this situation and place a (+) if they were positive and helpful and a (-) if they were negative and harmful.

What did you say, think, or do to try to address the feelings you were having?

Words -

Thoughts -

Actions -

Now write what you could have said, thought, or done differently to avoid having your feeling alert in the future.

Words -

Thoughts -

Actions -

Write an affirmation or God-power statement that could have been used to reverse and/or provide better coping skills when you first had your feeling alert during this situation.

CH 14: Emotions: Your Special Guide and Rudder – Part II

Briefly describe a situation where you *knew* you were **in danger** by the feelings you were experiencing. What were you doing, saying, or thinking that made you know something was wrong?

Describe all the feelings that you had relating to this situation and how you *knew* they were a warning.

List any thoughts that you remember having during this situation and place a (+) if they were positive and helpful and a (-) if they were negative and harmful.

What did you say, think, or do to try to address the feelings you were having?

Words -

Thoughts -

Actions -

Now write what you could have said, thought, or done differently to avoid having your feeling alert in the future.

Words -

Thoughts -

Actions -

Write an affirmation or God-power statement that could have been used to reverse and/or provide better coping skills when you first had your feeling alert during this situation.

CH 14: Emotions: Your Special Guide and Rudder – Part III-a

Briefly describe a difficult situation you encountered or are experiencing now.

List all the feelings that you had relating to this situation.

List the positive (+) and negative (-) elements related to the situation.

(+) Positive Elements   (-) Negative Elements

What are the worst possible outcomes this situation could lead to?

List any negative (-) thoughts you were having which enabled your negative (-) feelings to continue during this situation.

CH 14: Emotions: Your Special Guide and Rudder – Part III-b

What are the best case scenarios this situation can lead to?

List some positive (+) thoughts to use that will change the negative (-) feelings you are experiencing.

List the best ways you can think of to resolve this issue.

Now, take some time to think about each of these options, and try to get a sense of which choice *__feels__* right for you at this time. Then, explain your decision and reasoning for choosing this option below.

Next, create a God-power statement that connects you to your Source and helps you determine the best way to overcome and resolve this challenge and its accompanying emotions. (Example: Thank you God for your Divine guidance which leads to a practical resolution to my ordeal.) Then, take some time to quiet your mind and listen to your Divine guidance in order to discover if this agrees or disagrees with the way you want to resolve this issue.

CH 14: Dynamic Problem-Solving Through a Combined Approach
Part IV-a

1. Briefly describe the problem you wish to resolve:

2. List and then number all the available options for solving this problem:

3. After asking your Source for guidance and insights into this issue, take some time to ponder the positive (+) and negative (-) consequences for each of the better options you select. Then, use the boxes on the left to list your ideas. After asking your Source again for guidance and insights into this issue, take some quiet time to imagine and visualize yourself engaging in that specific decision and pay attention to how this feels. Then, record and rate your feelings afterward in the boxes on the right. Remember that each of the better options that you are processing involve two boxes which work together – one on the left and one on the right.

Option _____

Create a pros (+) and cons (-) list below for the option you identify.	Now list the positive (+) and negative (-) feelings you receive from visualizing this option.
(+) (+) (+) (-) (-) (-) Now rate your likelihood for using this option on a scale of (very unlikely) 1 – 10 (very likely) based on your pros and cons list. _____	(+) (+) (+) (-) (-) (-) After imagining this option, rate your overall feelings for this choice on a scale of (very negative) 1 – 10 (very positive). _____

CH 14: Dynamic Problem-Solving Through a Combined Approach
Part IV-b

Option _____

Create a pros (+) and cons (-) list below for the option you identify.

(+)
(+)
(+)

(-)
(-)
(-)

Now rate your likelihood for using this option on a scale of (very unlikely) 1 – 10 (very likely) based on your pros and cons list.

_____

Now list the positive (+) and negative (-) feelings you receive from visualizing this option.

(+)
(+)
(+)

(-)
(-)
(-)

After imagining this option, rate your overall feelings for this choice on a scale of (very negative) 1 – 10 (very positive).

_____

Option _____

Create a pros (+) and cons (-) list below for the option you identify.

(+)
(+)
(+)

(-)
(-)
(-)

Now rate your likelihood for using this option on a scale of (very unlikely) 1 – 10 (very likely) based on your pros and cons list.

_____

Now list the positive (+) and negative (-) feelings you receive from visualizing this option.

(+)
(+)
(+)

(-)
(-)
(-)

After imagining this option, rate your overall feelings for this choice on a scale of (very negative) 1 – 10 (very positive).

_____

---

4. Based on your use of rational thinking, feelings, and Divine guidance, indicate the best solution to the problem. Then, discuss your decision and reasoning for this solution below.

CH 14: Diamond Grid for Addressing Unfinished Emotional Baggage – Part V

1). Become aware whenever negative emotions emerge from within for no apparent reason. When this occurs, know that accumulated energy is being released from past pain which needs to be addressed. Part of acknowledging this pain is to know that any emotions you experience are separate from who you are as an individual; plus, you can control these rather than be controlled by them.

2). After noticing these emotions, take a few moments to feel and accept the fact that uncomfortable feelings have emerged. Then begin the practice of deep breathing immediately. Since emotions exist as they are, do not try to label these feelings as good or bad.

5). Instead, use a God-power statement or affirmation repeatedly to replace whatever thoughts are currently playing in your mind. One example to use is, "Thank you God for your Divine restoration's perfect work removing all negative emotions and underlying pain that is rooted deep within my body, mind, and spirit."

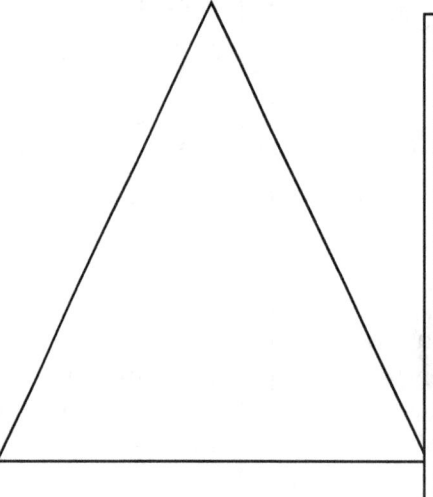

Remember: Uncomfortable Feelings and Emotions

3). Once you have acknowledged and felt the painful emotions, see yourself releasing them like balloons with every breath you exhale since they are no longer needed or welcome in your house and self. Using deeper breathing with symbolic imagery will lessen the power that negative emotions have over you the more you use it.

6). Such statements can be used individually or in combination with deeper breathing and visualization that could include cutting cords to emotional hurts with scissors or imagining a bunch of weeds, which represent emotional pain, being pulled out and cast into a purifying Violet Fire.

Result From

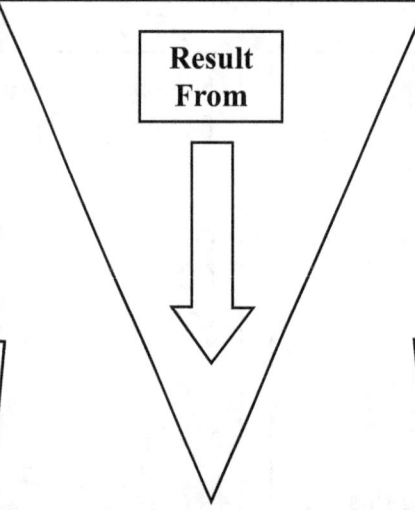

4). Whenever it arises, refuse to feed emotional pain with negative energy which is fueled by attention and thinking that replays hurtful interactions and/or events related to the poorer feelings you are experiencing.

Unfinished Business, the Pain-Body, and Emotional Baggage which are Names for the Same Underlying Emotional Pain.

Such Issues can be Fueled by Thoughts, Attention, Unconscious Memories, and Deeper Emotional Pain in Need of More Thorough Processing and Releasing.

7). Using this combination approach consistently will prevent the mind from replaying past hurtful events that feed lower emotions while simultaneously promoting a deeper, Divine cleansing. Plus, each time you engage in this process, you are diminishing the size and impact of your emotional baggage along with the fuel needed to sustain it.

CH 14: Releasing Negativity and Hurtful Emotions – Part VI-a

Use this worksheet to "let go" and release any anger, resentments, sadness, fear, and judgment in the form of negative thoughts, feelings, words, and/or behaviors you are holding within. If you are unsure what needs to be released or do not remember something, ask Divine guidance to help reveal this to you. Write what specifically needs to be released below since this is a very important step in the process of freeing up greater Divine energies within yourself.

I _____ (your name) now release all negativity in the following areas of my life:

In my words toward (specify):

In my thoughts about (specify):

In my feelings about (specify):

In my behaviors toward (specify):

CH 14: Releasing Negativity and Hurtful Emotions – Part VI-b

I _____ (your name) continue to release all negativity in the following areas of my life:

Additional people to be released involving (specify):

Additional events or situations to be released involving (specify):

Next, ask your Source to forgive the mistakes that you have made with others. List all the mistakes that you wish to be released and forgiven for now. Know that the moment you seek forgiveness it is granted to the extent that you are willing to forgive and release others.

Now, write a God-power statement that you will think and speak to help you release negativity as it connects you to higher Divine energies. As you consistently connect to your Source through the power of your words, this will assist you in the process of resolving your difficulties. Know that whenever you continuously turn your problems over to your Higher Power, everything will be resolved in the perfect time and way.

CH 14: Releasing Negativity and Lower Emotions Linked to the Unknown – Part VI-c

Unconscious thoughts and repressed memories linked to painful events can be another cause of the emotional pain, turmoil, and intrusive thoughts that people often experience, which also needs to be "let go." Using this healing imagery for 10 minutes each morning upon waking and just before bedtime will help to release and de-activate upsetting thoughts and lower emotions that can be tied to buried memories and other lower energies that continue to impact daily life.

1. Begin by calling upon the Almighty and the spiritual masters (i.e., holy ones, archangels, saints, ascended masters, etc.) you know of that possess healing abilities. Then, invite them into your protective bubble of expanding white light while you get into a more relaxed state of mind. Speaking or thinking words like, "Come Father-Mother God, ___, ___, and the Holy Spirit, you are welcome in this healing, cleansing, and release work" is one way to do this.

2. Now, imagine you are with these masters in a healing pool of light which has a powerful cleansing current that flows through you from head to toe. Deeply breathe in the Divine healing energies from this pool and slowly exhale whatever hinders this. Some people ask these master healers to hold their hands or place their hands of light on them to increase this revitalization.

3. Picture this powerful current of Divine Presence thoroughly cleansing your soul, body, mind, and spirit of any emotional pain, unconscious thoughts, and memories that are linked to the intrusive thoughts, harmful mindsets, lower feelings, and debilitating behaviors that you may be presently experiencing. Expect your healing to occur more and more every day.

4. Imagine, feel, hear, and picture all of this harmful residual negativity linked to unconscious memories, painful buried experiences, and any other forms of darkness that may have attached to your soul, body, mind, and spirit now being released in the form of darker bubbles that pop and dissolve as soon as they touch the powerful Divine healing light within this special pool.

5. Know that your soul in combination with these master healers truly desires to help you become healthy and whole. Best of all, this team will continue to do this special healing and cleansing work until it is completed, as you continue to use this imagery exercise and affirm throughout each day healing words such as, "Thank you Source, I AM being healed and cleansed all day in every way." Let these words take root within your spirit to enable Divine restoration to heal whatever has been buried and suppressed; then, see yourself as healed.

6. After you have allowed Divine Presence to thoroughly flush and cleanse you of all the darker bubbles that attached to all aspects of your being; then, imagine the Divine healing energies filling all bodily places and spaces from toe to head. Picture this amazing download continually providing you with every type of spiritual resource needed for your complete Divine healing, restoration, and wholeness to occur in the days, weeks, months, and years ahead.

7. Because you are now filled with higher spiritual energies, take a few moments to send this healing light to everyone you love and know, including those who you have offended and those who have offended you. Then, thank the master healers for their assistance and let them know you will return often to receive their healing energies. Your healing work will end when you no longer experience intrusive thoughts, lower feelings, and mindsets that emerge without a cause.

CHAPTER 15
Finding Your Passion and Purpose: Making the List – Part I-a

List all of your interests, hobbies, and activities, and particularly those that you enjoy doing the most.

Now rank these interests in the order from most to least preferred.

1.
2.
3.
4.
5.
6.
7.
8.
9.
10.
11.
12.

CH 15: Finding Your Passion and Purpose: Making the List – Part I-b

Write a brief summary of what a day in your life would be like while working in your perfect occupation – without mentioning what that occupation is. Be specific and include as many details about your life covering as many areas as possible.

CH 15: Narrowing Decisions for Occupations:
Compare and Contrast – Part II-a

Now choose the first of your three favorite interests and activities from the previous list which you could see yourself doing and enjoying as a future occupation. Then, complete the following worksheets (a-f) for each occupation which will help you to narrow your list from three potential occupations to only one.

1st Occupation:

List all the positive reasons for wanting to do this occupation, and all the negative reasons that would prevent you from wanting to do this as an occupation. Be as detailed as possible.

Write This List of Positives (+) Below	**Write This List of Negatives (-) Below**

After making a careful and complete comparison of the positives and negatives of this occupation, now rate your feelings regarding this occupation:

Excellent / Very Good / Good / Fair / Poor / Very Poor

CH 15: Narrowing Decisions for Occupations: Considering Holistic Concerns – Part II-b

1st Occupation:

1. Describe how this occupation will satisfy your physical self. (i.e., How demanding will the work be on your overall body and health? How much physical work is required for this position and is it too little or too much? Are you able to live on the salary from this work?)

Rate the importance of this aspect of the self – High   5   4   3   2   1   Low

2. Describe how this occupation will satisfy your mental/intellectual self. (i.e., How will this work impact your mental health? How will you be challenged and intellectually stimulated in this position? Are you over or under qualified for this type of work? Is there opportunity for advancement and continued learning or is stagnation likely to happen?)

Rate the importance of this aspect of the self – High   5   4   3   2   1   Low

3. Describe how this occupation will satisfy your emotional/feeling self. (i.e., How will the tasks required in this occupation impact your feelings and emotional self? What elements of this work in particular will increase or decrease the feelings you experience and the way you feel about your overall self?)

Rate the importance of this aspect of the self – High   5   4   3   2   1   Low

CH 15: Narrowing Decisions for Occupations: Considering Holistic Concerns – Part II-c

1st Occupation:

4. Describe how this occupation satisfies your energetic self (i.e., How stressful do you anticipate this occupation to be? What do you see as the major energy enhancers and reducers linked to this occupation? How will you manage and conserve your energy in this position?)

Rate the importance of this aspect of the self – High   5   4   3   2   1   Low

5. Describe how this occupation satisfies your relational self (i.e., How much interaction with others is required in this position? How much independence versus team interaction do you desire in an occupation? How do you rate your interpersonal and conflict resolution skills?)

Rate the importance of this aspect of the self – High   5   4   3   2   1   Low

6. Describe how this occupation satisfies your spiritual self. (i.e., How might this occupation challenge, enhance, or compromise your spiritual and ethical qualities? How will this position enable you to be of service to others using your special gifts and talents?) Remember: Higher purpose work always involves spiritual resources that enable your skills to supersede your own capabilities.

Rate the importance of this aspect of the self – High   5   4   3   2   1   Low

CH 15: Narrowing Decisions for Occupations: Looking at Details – Part II-d

1st Occupation: Briefly discuss your primary motives for wanting to do this occupation:

1a. Using a scale of 1-10, circle the number reflecting **the amount of effort** you are willing put into achieving this occupation.

Low Effort 1 2 3 4 5 6 7 8 9 10 **High Effort**

1b. Next, circle how much **desire and passion** you have for this line of work.

Low Desire/Passion 1 2 3 4 5 6 7 8 9 10 **High Desire/Passion**

2. Describe any special training or education needed in this occupation.

3. Describe specific and daily behaviors that are essential for success when working in this occupation.

4. Describe the specific type of mindset that is essential for success when working in this occupation.

5. Describe the daily spiritual practices that will promote success when working in this occupation.

6. List those who will support you in achieving this occupation, and briefly describe how they can help.

CH 15: Narrowing Decisions for Occupations: Divine Guidance Method (DGM) Part II-e

1. Completing all of the exercises on the previous pages for each of your potential occupations will give you a better understanding, analysis, and feel for what you may or may not want to pursue, however, this is not enough.

2. To summon help from your inner guidance by asking for divine occupational assistance, begin by speaking a detailed God-power statement such as,

"Thank you God I AM in my true place in life doing the work I AM meant for which gives me tremendous peace and satisfaction. I AM grateful to be able to share my unique talents with the world in remarkable ways. Thank you for wonderful opportunities that are opening up for me to serve others in more active and impacting ways which provides me with increasing prosperity in the process. Thank you that I AM divinely guided, protected, directed, prospered, and blessed in all that I do to my highest good and expression. As a child of God, I know that I AM endowed with all the powers and qualities of my Source. I know I can do all things through the Divine Presence within that strengthens me because if God is with me, who or what can be against me?"

3. After repeating the above statement several times while holding the worksheets for a particular occupation in your hand, begin to imagine, visualize, and feel what it is like to be in this special position. Continue with this imagery for about five minutes.

4. Now, see yourself sitting in a protective bubble of Divine white light with your spiritual guides and masters while engaging in deeper breathing. As you do this, begin to still your thoughts and mind. You are now moving into listening mode which is similar to what occurs in quiet meditation since this uses no thinking, only silence. As your mind becomes quiet and still for at least five minutes, be alert to the types of thoughts and feelings you are receiving about this specific occupation. You may or may not receive information immediately, however, it is not essential to receive guidance in that specific moment. Just know that whenever you seek guidance and awareness that it will be revealed in time and particularly when you continue to put your mind into more receptive states (i.e., listening mode) for receiving information. Feel free to consult the chapter on meditation to get more information on this practice if you need to.

5. Continue to repeat the above process each day for as long as you are seeking information. Know that the guidance will often arrive through thoughts, feelings, and ideas that come from within your own mind and thinking. Sometimes the guidance will be revealed through a book, person, or something that you hear about. Be sure to keep your eyes and ears open for synchronistic occurrences and answers to your questions from any number of sources.

6. When you receive information that gives you a sense of deeper peace and knowing, then it is important to follow that guidance and act on it. Receiving messages that provide an inner sense of peace and certainty is how you will know you are connecting to the Divine guidance you have been seeking from the highest Source.

CH 15: Narrowing Decisions for Occupations: Divine Guidance Method (DGM) Part II-f

7. Once you use this method for a period of time, you will be able to compare the Divine guidance and information you are receiving for each of the different occupations individually as well as when comparing the occupations side-by-side. This will give you a better sense of direction for your choices. Remember that using shorter God-power statements such as: "Thank you God for Divine guidance that is revealing my perfect occupation at this time" will help to prevent negative thinking and doubt from undoing your desires and pursuits while you go about your day.

8. Using this approach is very useful since it comes from the highest Source in ways that supersede reason and logic. Because there are so many behind-the-scene aspects to an occupation that we can never know about until we are in a certain position, using the Divine Guidance Method (DGM) can assist in leading us to our proper place in ways that we could never achieve by ourselves. Remember that Divine law is activated whenever we ask and seek for Divine guidance, and this will result in finding answers and doors being opened. Trust in the process as well as your Source to provide answers from the highest guidance and good that is available.

Now in the space below, describe any insights and information from the thoughts, feelings, and intuition that you have received concerning the occupation you are asking about. What are you learning and what do you feel is being revealed to you?

CH 15: Narrowing Decisions for Occupations: Compare and Contrast – Part III-a

Now choose the second of your three favorite interests and activities from the previous list which you could see yourself doing and enjoying as a future occupation. Then, complete the following worksheets (a-f) for each occupation which will help you to narrow your list from three potential occupations to only one.

2nd Occupation:

List all the positive reasons for wanting to do this occupation, and all the negative reasons that would prevent you from wanting to do this as an occupation. Be as detailed as possible.

Write This List of Positives (+) Below	**Write This List of Negatives (-) Below**

After making a careful and complete comparison of the positives and negatives of this occupation, now rate your feelings regarding this occupation:

Excellent / Very Good / Good / Fair / Poor / Very Poor

CH 15: Narrowing Decisions for Occupations: Considering Holistic Concerns – Part III-b

2nd Occupation:

1. Describe how this occupation will satisfy your physical self. (i.e., How demanding will the work be on your overall body and health? How much physical work is required for this position and is it too little or too much? Are you able to live on the salary from this work?)

Rate the importance of this aspect of the self – High   5   4   3   2   1   Low

2. Describe how this occupation will satisfy your mental/intellectual self. (i.e., How will this work impact your mental health? How will you be challenged and intellectually stimulated in this position? Are you over or under qualified for this type of work? Is there opportunity for advancement and continued learning or is stagnation likely to happen?)

Rate the importance of this aspect of the self – High   5   4   3   2   1   Low

3. Describe how this occupation will satisfy your emotional/feeling self. (i.e., How will the tasks required in this occupation impact your feelings and emotional self? What elements of this work in particular will increase or decrease the feelings you experience and the way you feel about your overall self?)

Rate the importance of this aspect of the self – High   5   4   3   2   1   Low

Chapter 15 - Finding Passion and Purpose

CH 15: Narrowing Decisions for Occupations: Considering Holistic Concerns – Part III-c

2nd Occupation:

4. Describe how this occupation satisfies your energetic self (i.e., How stressful do you anticipate this occupation to be? What do you see as the major energy enhancers and reducers linked to this occupation? How will you manage and conserve your energy in this position?)

Rate the importance of this aspect of the self – High   5   4   3   2   1   Low

5. Describe how this occupation satisfies your relational self (i.e., How much interaction with others is required in this position? How much independence versus team interaction do you desire in an occupation? How do you rate your interpersonal and conflict resolution skills?)

Rate the importance of this aspect of the self – High   5   4   3   2   1   Low

6. Describe how this occupation satisfies your spiritual self. (i.e., How might this occupation challenge, enhance, or compromise your spiritual and ethical qualities? How will this position enable you to be of service to others using your special gifts and talents?) Remember: Higher purpose work always involves spiritual resources that enable your skills to supersede your own capabilities.

Rate the importance of this aspect of the self – High   5   4   3   2   1   Low

CH 15: Narrowing Decisions for Occupations: Looking at Details – Part III-d

2nd Occupation: Briefly discuss your primary motives for wanting to do this occupation:

1a. Using a scale of 1-10, circle the number reflecting the **amount of effort** you are willing put into achieving this occupation.

Low Effort 1 2 3 4 5 6 7 8 9 10 **High Effort**

1b. Next, circle how much **desire and passion** you have for this line of work.

Low Desire/Passion 1 2 3 4 5 6 7 8 9 10 **High Desire/Passion**

2. Describe any special training or education needed in this occupation.

3. Describe specific and daily behaviors that are essential for success when working in this occupation.

4. Describe the specific type of mindset that is essential for success when working in this occupation.

5. Describe the daily spiritual practices that will promote success when working in this occupation.

6. List those who will support you in achieving this occupation, and briefly describe how they can help.

CH 15: Narrowing Decisions for Occupations: Divine Guidance Method (DGM) Part III-e

1. Completing all of the exercises on the previous pages for each of your potential occupations will give you a better understanding, analysis, and feel for what you may or may not want to pursue, however, this is not enough.

2. To summon help from your inner guidance by asking for divine occupational assistance, begin by speaking a detailed God-power statement such as,

"Thank you God I AM in my true place in life doing the work I AM meant for which gives me tremendous peace and satisfaction. I AM grateful to be able to share my unique talents with the world in remarkable ways. Thank you for wonderful opportunities that are opening up for me to serve others in more active and impacting ways which provides me with increasing prosperity in the process. Thank you that I AM divinely guided, protected, directed, prospered, and blessed in all that I do to my highest good and expression. As a child of God, I know that I AM endowed with all the powers and qualities of my Source. I know I can do all things through the Divine Presence within that strengthens me because if God is with me, who or what can be against me?"

3. After repeating the above statement several times while holding the worksheets for a particular occupation in your hand, begin to imagine, visualize, and feel what it is like to be in this special position. Continue with this imagery for about five minutes.

4. Now, see yourself sitting in a protective bubble of Divine white light with your spiritual guides and masters while engaging in deeper breathing. As you do this, begin to still your thoughts and mind. You are now moving into listening mode which is similar to what occurs in quiet meditation since this uses no thinking, only silence. As your mind becomes quiet and still for at least five minutes, be alert to the types of thoughts and feelings you are receiving about this specific occupation. You may or may not receive information immediately, however, it is not essential to receive guidance in that specific moment. Just know that whenever you seek guidance and awareness that it will be revealed in time and particularly when you continue to put your mind into more receptive states (i.e., listening mode) for receiving information. Feel free to consult the chapter on meditation to get more information on this practice if you need to.

5. Continue to repeat the above process each day for as long as you are seeking information. Know that the guidance will often arrive through thoughts, feelings, and ideas that come from within your own mind and thinking. Sometimes the guidance will be revealed through a book, person, or something that you hear about. Be sure to keep your eyes and ears open for synchronistic occurrences and answers to your questions from any number of sources.

6. When you receive information that gives you a sense of deeper peace and knowing, then it is important to follow that guidance and act on it. Receiving messages that provide an inner sense of peace and certainty is how you will know you are connecting to the Divine guidance you have been seeking from the highest Source.

CH 15: Narrowing Decisions for Occupations: Divine Guidance Method (DGM) Part III-f

7. Once you use this method for a period of time, you will be able to compare the Divine guidance and information you are receiving for each of the different occupations individually as well as when comparing the occupations side-by-side. This will give you a better sense of direction for your choices. Remember that using shorter God-power statements such as: "Thank you God for Divine guidance that is revealing my perfect occupation at this time" will help to prevent negative thinking and doubt from undoing your desires and pursuits while you go about your day.

8. Using this approach is very useful since it comes from the highest Source in ways that supersede reason and logic. Because there are so many behind-the-scene aspects to an occupation that we can never know about until we are in a certain position, using the Divine Guidance Method (DGM) can assist in leading us to our proper place in ways that we could never achieve by ourselves. Remember that Divine law is activated whenever we ask and seek for Divine guidance, and this will result in finding answers and doors being opened. Trust in the process as well as your Source to provide answers from the highest guidance and good that is available.

Now in the space below, describe any insights and information from the thoughts, feelings, and intuition that you have received concerning the occupation you are asking about. What are you learning and what do you feel is being revealed to you?

CH 15: Narrowing Decisions for Occupations: Compare and Contrast – Part IV-a

Now choose the third of your three favorite interests and activities from the previous list which you could see yourself doing and enjoying as a future occupation. Then, complete the following worksheets (a-f) for each occupation which will help you to narrow your list from three potential occupations to only one.

3rd Occupation:

List all the positive reasons for wanting to do this occupation, and all the negative reasons that would prevent you from wanting to do this as an occupation. Be as detailed as possible.

Write This List of Positives (+) Below

Write This List of Negatives (-) Below

After making a careful and complete comparison of the positives and negatives of this occupation, now rate your feelings regarding this occupation:

Excellent / Very Good / Good / Fair / Poor / Very Poor

CH 15: Narrowing Decisions for Occupations: Considering Holistic Concerns – Part IV-b

3rd Occupation:

1. Describe how this occupation will satisfy your physical self. (i.e., How demanding will the work be on your overall body and health? How much physical work is required for this position and is it too little or too much? Are you able to live on the salary from this work?)

Rate the importance of this aspect of the self – High   5   4   3   2   1   Low

2. Describe how this occupation will satisfy your mental/intellectual self. (i.e., How will this work impact your mental health? How will you be challenged and intellectually stimulated in this position? Are you over or under qualified for this type of work? Is there opportunity for advancement and continued learning or is stagnation likely to happen?)

Rate the importance of this aspect of the self – High   5   4   3   2   1   Low

3. Describe how this occupation will satisfy your emotional/feeling self. (i.e., How will the tasks required in this occupation impact your feelings and emotional self? What elements of this work in particular will increase or decrease the feelings you experience and the way you feel about your overall self?)

Rate the importance of this aspect of the self – High   5   4   3   2   1   Low

CH 15: Narrowing Decisions for Occupations: Considering Holistic Concerns – Part IV-c

3rd Occupation:

4. Describe how this occupation satisfies your energetic self (i.e., How stressful do you anticipate this occupation to be? What do you see as the major energy enhancers and reducers linked to this occupation? How will you manage and conserve your energy in this position?)

Rate the importance of this aspect of the self – High   5   4   3   2   1   Low

5. Describe how this occupation satisfies your relational self (i.e., How much interaction with others is required in this position? How much independence versus team interaction do you desire in an occupation? How do you rate your interpersonal and conflict resolution skills?)

Rate the importance of this aspect of the self – High   5   4   3   2   1   Low

6. Describe how this occupation satisfies your spiritual self. (i.e., How might this occupation challenge, enhance, or compromise your spiritual and ethical qualities? How will this position enable you to be of service to others using your special gifts and talents?) Remember: Higher purpose work always involves spiritual resources that enable your skills to supersede your own capabilities.

Rate the importance of this aspect of the self – High   5   4   3   2   1   Low

CH 15: Narrowing Decisions for Occupations: Looking at Details – Part IV-d

3rd Occupation: Briefly discuss your primary motives for wanting to do this occupation:

1a. Using a scale of 1-10, circle the number reflecting **the amount of effort** you are willing put into achieving this occupation.

Low Effort 1 2 3 4 5 6 7 8 9 10 **High Effort**

1b. Next, circle how much **desire and passion** you have for this line of work.

Low Desire/Passion 1 2 3 4 5 6 7 8 9 10 **High Desire/Passion**

2. Describe any special training or education needed in this occupation.

3. Describe specific and daily behaviors that are essential for success when working in this occupation.

4. Describe the specific type of mindset that is essential for success when working in this occupation.

5. Describe the daily spiritual practices that will promote success when working in this occupation.

6. List those who will support you in achieving this occupation, and briefly describe how they can help.

CH 15: Narrowing Decisions for Occupations: Divine Guidance Method (DGM) Part IV-e

1. Completing all of the exercises on the previous pages for each of your potential occupations will give you a better understanding, analysis, and feel for what you may or may not want to pursue, however, this is not enough.

2. To summon help from your inner guidance by asking for divine occupational assistance, begin by speaking a detailed God-power statement such as,

"Thank you God I AM in my true place in life doing the work I AM meant for which gives me tremendous peace and satisfaction. I AM grateful to be able to share my unique talents with the world in remarkable ways. Thank you for wonderful opportunities that are opening up for me to serve others in more active and impacting ways which provides me with increasing prosperity in the process. Thank you that I AM divinely guided, protected, directed, prospered, and blessed in all that I do to my highest good and expression. As a child of God, I know that I AM endowed with all the powers and qualities of my Source. I know I can do all things through the Divine Presence within that strengthens me because if God is with me, who or what can be against me?"

3. After repeating the above statement several times while holding the worksheets for a particular occupation in your hand, begin to imagine, visualize, and feel what it is like to be in this special position. Continue with this imagery for about five minutes.

4. Now, see yourself sitting in a protective bubble of Divine white light with your spiritual guides and masters while engaging in deeper breathing. As you do this, begin to still your thoughts and mind. You are now moving into listening mode which is similar to what occurs in quiet meditation since this uses no thinking, only silence. As your mind becomes quiet and still for at least five minutes, be alert to the types of thoughts and feelings you are receiving about this specific occupation. You may or may not receive information immediately, however, it is not essential to receive guidance in that specific moment. Just know that whenever you seek guidance and awareness that it will be revealed in time and particularly when you continue to put your mind into more receptive states (i.e., listening mode) for receiving information. Feel free to consult the chapter on meditation to get more information on this practice if you need to.

5. Continue to repeat the above process each day for as long as you are seeking information. Know that the guidance will often arrive through thoughts, feelings, and ideas that come from within your own mind and thinking. Sometimes the guidance will be revealed through a book, person, or something that you hear about. Be sure to keep your eyes and ears open for synchronistic occurrences and answers to your questions from any number of sources.

6. When you receive information that gives you a sense of deeper peace and knowing, then it is important to follow that guidance and act on it. Receiving messages that provide an inner sense of peace and certainty is how you will know you are connecting to the Divine guidance you have been seeking from the highest Source.

CH 15: Narrowing Decisions for Occupations: Divine Guidance Method (DGM) Part IV-f

7. Once you use this method for a period of time, you will be able to compare the Divine guidance and information you are receiving for each of the different occupations individually as well as when comparing the occupations side-by-side. This will give you a better sense of direction for your choices. Remember that using shorter God-power statements such as: "Thank you God for Divine guidance that is revealing my perfect occupation at this time" will help to prevent negative thinking and doubt from undoing your desires and pursuits while you go about your day.

8. Using this approach is very useful since it comes from the highest Source in ways that supersede reason and logic. Because there are so many behind-the-scene aspects to an occupation that we can never know about until we are in a certain position, using the Divine Guidance Method (DGM) can assist in leading us to our proper place in ways that we could never achieve by ourselves. Remember that Divine law is activated whenever we ask and seek for Divine guidance, and this will result in finding answers and doors being opened. Trust in the process as well as your Source to provide answers from the highest guidance and good that is available.

Now in the space below, describe any insights and information from the thoughts, feelings, and intuition that you have received concerning the occupation you are asking about. What are you learning and what do you feel is being revealed to you?

CH 15: Moving Toward Change in Your Present Work – Part V-a

1. List the concerns you have in your current occupation or activity:

2. Using a scale of 1-10, circle the number reflecting your **past effort level** in this occupation (i.e., how hard you try at work) compared to the **present effort level** you have now for this work or activity.

Past Effort

    1 2 3 4 5 6 7 8 9 10
  (very little)   (very much)

Present Effort

    1 2 3 4 5 6 7 8 9 10
  (very little)   (very much)

3. List three possible reasons for any change in your effort now at work:

4. Using a scale of 1-10, circle the number reflecting your **past passion level** for this occupation (i.e., how much you enjoy it) compared to the **current passion level** you have now for this work or activity.

Past Passion

    1 2 3 4 5 6 7 8 9 10
  (very little)   (very much)

Present Passion

    1 2 3 4 5 6 7 8 9 10
  (very little)   (very much)

CH 15: Moving Toward Change in Your Present Work – Part V-b

5. List three possible reasons for any changes in the level of passion you have for your present work or activity:

6. List the thoughts, feelings, and/or inner promptings which suggest it may be time for a change in work:

7. How long have you had these thoughts, feelings, or inner promptings and what do you believe is at the root of these messages?

8. How strong are these thoughts, feelings, or inner promptings? (High) 5 4 3 2 1 (Low) Explain.

CH 15: Moving Toward Change in Your Present Work – Part V-c

1. List three things that would prevent you from leaving your current occupation or activity.

2. List three ways you can overcome the obstacles you have listed.

3. How soon will you be ready to change to a new and more rewarding mission, purpose, and work?

(Not Ready Yet)   1 2 3 4 5 6 7 8 9 10   (Very Ready)

4. How strongly do you want to change to a new and more rewarding mission, purpose, and work?

(Not Ready Yet)   1 2 3 4 5 6 7 8 9 10   (Very Strongly)

5. Describe specific and daily behaviors that are essential for helping you to leave your present occupation for a new mission, purpose, and work.

6. Describe the daily thinking and mindset that is essential for helping you to leave your present occupation for a new mission, purpose, and work.

7. Describe the daily spiritual practices that are essential for helping you to leave your present occupation and find a new mission, purpose, and work.

8. List those who will support you in this transition, and describe how they can help.

CH 15: Attracting a New Occupation – Part VI

1. The following exercise is a very powerful and effective way to seed your soul, body, mind, and spirit with uplifting information each day which will help you attract and connect with what you desire. Take 8-12 minutes several times each day and especially upon waking in the morning and just before falling asleep at night since the deeper mind and powerful "being" self are very relaxed and open to suggestion at these times. Performing this exercise consistently will enable your uplifting words to take root and manifest more readily your life.

The following is an example of one such script you can use although it is best to personalize this information with your own words once you are accustomed to performing this practice.

> *Thank you God I AM in my true place in life doing the work I AM destined for which gives me tremendous peace and satisfaction. I AM grateful to be able to share my unique talents with the world in remarkable ways. Thank you for wonderful opportunities that are opening up for me to serve others in more active and impacting ways which provides me with increasing prosperity in the process. Thank you that I AM divinely guided, protected, directed, safe, secure, and blessed in all that I do to my highest good and expression. I know that as a child of God, I AM endowed with all the powers and qualities of my Source. I know I can do all things through the God Power within that strengthens me because if God is with me, who or what can be against me? Only good things happen to me as I AM being directed and blessed more and more every day in every way. Thank you I AM protected, healed, awakened, restored, and guided every day in every way. I thank you that I AM fulfilling the purposes of God's plan for my life every day.*

3. After using the above God-power statement for at least five minutes while holding thoughts about the particular occupation you would like to do, begin imagining and visualizing yourself being congratulated by others for achieving this occupation. Be sure to actually feel what it is like to be in this special position. Continue with this imagery for at least another five minutes.

4. Continue to repeat the above process several times each day until you connect with your divinely-appointed occupation. Remember that using shorter God-power statements such as: "Thank you God I AM connecting to my special occupation in Divine order and perfection" will help to prevent negative thinking and doubt from undoing your desires and pursuits while going about your day.

5. Know that the guidance and information you are seeking often arrive through thoughts, feelings, and ideas that come from within your own mind and thinking. At other times, the guidance may be revealed through a book, person, or something that you hear about. Keep your eyes and ears open for synchronistic occurrences and answers pertaining to your pursuit and questions from any number of sources.

6. Finally, trust in the process knowing that your Higher Power will do its part to provide the guidance and gifts you seek with perfect timing and in ways that we could never accomplish by ourselves.

CHAPTER 16

Activating and Allowing Greater Flow Before an Event – Part I-a

Examine the recharging activities that you will use to prepare for an event or performance.

1. Am I able to take a power nap to recharge before this event? Yes___ No___ If yes…

Where can you do this?

When can you do this?

How long do you have for this?

If not…

2. Am I able to find a quiet place to ready myself before an event? Yes___ No___ If yes…

Where can you do this?

When can you do this?

How long do you have for this?

3. Am I able to use some visualization, dynamic relaxation, and/or deep 3-second breathing to recharge and ready myself before an event? Yes___ No___

Briefly describe your choice and rationale for using one of these methods or declining them.

Where can you do this?

When can you do this?

How long do you have for this?

4. If the above methods are not doable or to your liking, take some time to think about what tools you will use to occupy and/or distract the mind to conserve energy before an event. Then, continue with the second part of this exercise.

CH 16: Activating and Allowing Greater Flow
Before an Event – Part I-b

5. Identify some of the ways you will occupy your mind to conserve energy before an event.

___ I will listen to some "high vibe" music to occupy and/or distract my mind before an event.

___ I will unwind with some light reading to occupy my mind before an event.

___ I will unwind with light television or _____ to occupy my mind before an event.

___ I will unwind with some light physical activity, such as stretching, taking a short walk, or practicing deep breathing, to occupy and/or distract my mind before an event.

___ I will connect with Source Energy to prepare and focus my mind before an event.

6. List some other preferred ways to ready yourself before an event, which also enables you to keep your mind occupied before an event. List and briefly note how these tools will help you.

If these methods fail…

7. List some additional steps you will take to prepare yourself and address any negative or stressful thinking if your mind begins to drain your energies before an event.

8. List the people you can talk to that can help ready you and especially if the mind begins to drain your energies before an event.

CH 16: Activating and Allowing Greater Flow During an Event – Part II-a

Discuss the recharging activities you plan to use during an event or performance.

1. Am I prepared with a specific visualization or imagery that will enable me to recharge during an event? Yes___ No___ If yes, describe this below and if no, discuss your reasoning for this.

2. Am I prepared with a variety of silent power words that will allow me to recharge during an event? Yes___ No___ If yes, write these below and if no, discuss your reasoning for this.

3. Am I prepared with different silent power phrases that will allow me to recharge during an event? Yes___ No___ If yes, write these below and if no, discuss your reasoning for this.

4. Am I prepared with several silent affirmations that will allow me to recharge during an event? Yes___ No___ If yes, write these below and if no, discuss your reasoning for this.

CH 16: Activating and Allowing Greater Flow During an Event – Part II-b

Discuss the recharging activities you plan to use during an event or performance.

5. Am I prepared with silent spiritual affirmations or God-power statements that will allow me to recharge during an event? If yes, write these below and if no, discuss your reasoning for this.

6. Am I prepared to use the "no thinking" method that will enable me to stay in-the-moment to recharge during an event? Yes___ No___ If yes, describe how you plan to do this below, and if no, discuss your reasoning for this.

7. Am I using deeper 3-second breathing techniques in combination with any of the above methods to recharge during an event? Yes___ No___ If yes, briefly discuss your use of this below and if no, discuss your reasoning for this.

8. Describe your preferred method from those listed above or from another technique that you have found most useful for recharging in-the-moment during an event or performance.

CH 16: Activating and Allowing Greater Flow After an Event and for Life – Part III-a

Daily Food Journaling

Day_____   Date_____

Keeping a food journal of what you eat each day is a great way to examine the foods you eat as well as those that should be replaced with healthier options. Healthier food choices always provide more energy and healing than less healthy options. Strive to make one healthy food substitution each week that you will continue to maintain. Remember to bless all your food before eating to increase the food's positive energy and impact.

                              Foods Eaten Today   **Healthier Food Substitutions**

Breakfast

Morning Snack

Lunch

Afternoon Snack

Dinner

Evening Snack

Approximate Calories for the day_____

Discuss any thoughts and feelings about your day in relation to the food you ate, including the new healthy food choices you made today.

CH 16: Activating and Allowing Greater Flow After an Event and for Life – Part III-b

Weekly Food Journal from _____ **to** _____

	MONDAY ___/___/__	TUESDAY ___/___/__	WEDNESDAY ___/___/__	THURSDAY ___/___/__	FRIDAY ___/___/__	SATURDAY ___/___/__
Breakfast						
Snack						
Lunch						
Snack						
Dinner						
Snack						
Daily Calorie Intake:	_____	_____	_____	_____	_____	_____

List this week's healthier food substitutions:

CH 16: Activating and Allowing Greater Flow After an Event and for Life – Part III-c

Monthly Sleep and Rest Log

Keeping a sleep and rest log will help you examine the days and nights that cause energy depletion, so you can take steps to increase the quality and/or quantity of your sleep and rest. Record the number of hours you sleep each night below for a particular month and be sure to make appropriate changes as needed knowing that 6-8 hours per day are optimal.

MONDAY	TUESDAY	WEDNESDAY	THURSDAY	FRIDAY	SATURDAY	SUNDAY

Next, write a pre-sleep statement or visualization to assist you in making the most out of the time that you spend sleeping. List any other strategies that promote positive sleep preparation.

Record the amount of time that you use to rest and rejuvenate each day for a particular month.

MONDAY	TUESDAY	WEDNESDAY	THURSDAY	FRIDAY	SATURDAY	SUNDAY

Then, list the energy enhancement strategies you will use to assist in making the most out of the time that you spend rejuvenating and recharging your energies each day.

CH 16: Activating and Allowing Greater Flow After an Event and for Life – Part III-d

Monthly Exercise and Workout Log

Record the amount of time you spend exercising each day for a particular month. Be sure to make appropriate changes as needed knowing that at least 30 minutes per day is essential.

MONDAY	TUESDAY	WEDNESDAY	THURSDAY	FRIDAY	SATURDAY	SUNDAY

Now record the types of exercises that you are doing each day for a particular month. Be sure to consult the worksheets from the stress-busting chapter which provide energizing exercises and a variety of excellent workout plans.

MONDAY	
TUESDAY	
WEDNESDAY	
THURSDAY	
FRIDAY	
SATURDAY	
SUNDAY	

Then list the power words, phrases, affirmations, and/or visualizations that you will use to energize and help to make the most out of the time that you spend exercising.

CH 16: Activating and Allowing Greater Flow
After an Event and for Life – Part III-e

Monthly Exercise and Workout Log

MONDAY	
TUESDAY	
WEDNESDAY	
THURSDAY	
FRIDAY	
SATURDAY	
SUNDAY	

MONDAY	
TUESDAY	
WEDNESDAY	
THURSDAY	
FRIDAY	
SATURDAY	
SUNDAY	

List the power words, phrases, affirmations, and/or visualizations that you will use to energize and help to make the most out of the time that you spend exercising.

CH 16: Activating and Allowing Greater Flow After an Event and for Life – Part III-f

Monthly Exercise and Workout Log

MONDAY	
TUESDAY	
WEDNESDAY	
THURSDAY	
FRIDAY	
SATURDAY	
SUNDAY	

MONDAY	
TUESDAY	
WEDNESDAY	
THURSDAY	
FRIDAY	
SATURDAY	
SUNDAY	

List the power words, phrases, affirmations, and/or visualizations that you will use to energize and help to make the most out of the time that you spend exercising.

CH 16: Daily Workout Log – Part III-g

Day_____   Date_____

List Exercises: As part of a warm-up:_____minutes. As part of a cool down:_____minutes.

Cardio and Interval Exercises: Record as minutes, number of miles, or intervals completed.

Running_____   Walking_____   Elliptical_____   Glide Board_____   Rowing_____

Cycling_____   Aerobics_____   Stairclimbing_____   Other_____   Swimming_____

Strength Training Exercises:

1). Exercise Performed:_____   **2). Exercise Performed:**_____

Set 1 _____Weight_____Reps:_____   Set 1 _____Weight_____Reps:_____

Set 2 _____Weight_____Reps:_____   Set 2 _____Weight_____Reps:_____

Set 3 _____Weight_____Reps:_____   Set 3 _____Weight_____Reps:_____

3). Exercise Performed:_____   **4). Exercise Performed:**_____

Set 1 _____Weight_____Reps:_____   Set 1 _____Weight_____Reps:_____

Set 2 _____Weight_____Reps:_____   Set 2 _____Weight_____Reps:_____

Set 3 _____Weight_____Reps:_____   Set 3 _____Weight_____Reps:_____

5). Exercise Performed:_____   **6). Exercise Performed:**_____

Set 1 _____Weight_____Reps:_____   Set 1 _____Weight_____Reps:_____

Set 2 _____Weight_____Reps:_____   Set 2 _____Weight_____Reps:_____

Set 3 _____Weight_____Reps:_____   Set 3 _____Weight_____Reps:_____

7). Exercise Performed:_____   **8). Exercise Performed:**_____

Set 1 _____Weight_____Reps:_____   Set 1 _____Weight_____Reps:_____

Set 2 _____Weight_____Reps:_____   Set 2 _____Weight_____Reps:_____

Set 3 _____Weight_____Reps:_____   Set 3 _____Weight_____Reps:_____

9). Abdominal Exercises: Sets/Reps_____   **10). Back Raises:** Sets/Reps_____

_____: Sets/Reps_____   _____: Sets/Reps_____

CH 16: Activating and Allowing Greater Flow After an Event and for Life – Part III-h

Three-Column "To Do" List

Making your three-column "to do" list will help you to organize and prioritize the tasks you need to complete within a day, week, or monthly time period. Be sure to focus on one task at a time beginning with the most pressing work each day. Don't forget to ask for Divine assistance and guidance which stands ready to help in all matters, but only when assistance is requested by setting your intention.

High Priority Tasks	**Medium Priority Tasks**	**Low Priority Tasks**

CH 16: Activating and Allowing Greater Flow After an Event and for Life – Part III-i

Diamond Grid for Improving Energy Flow

1). Briefly describe a challenging event that required more energy than you had available:

2). List the energy-enhancing methods below that you have used in the past which were unsuccessful during the above event.

5). Now list all the new methods you are willing to use to effectively overcome this event and any other depleting factors in the space below.

3). List any negative (-) thinking or feelings below that resulted from your lack of success.

Remember: Uplifting Thoughts in Mindsets with Positive Emotions Combine with Activating and Allowing Actions That…

Increase

6). Based on your new plan of action, list the top three methods that have brought you the most favorable results.

4). Because all types of negativity further deplete energy flow in addition to the event itself, begin thinking about your plan of action to address this.

Energy Flow in You

7). Since empowered actions, thoughts, and feelings increase energy flow in time, be sure to continue on this uplifting course.

208 *Discovering Your Excellence Within Workbook*

CH 16: Activating and Allowing Greater Flow After an Event and for Life – Part III-j

Addressing Energy Leaks to Improve Energy and Flow

Briefly describe a situation in your life that you feel is draining your energy. Then, rate the leak on a scale of 1-3 with 1 being a minor energy leak, 2 being a medium-level energy leak, and 3 being a major energy leak. Be sure to examine areas such as work, school, sports, family, friendships, intimate partnerships, and any other relationships. Then answer the questions below to address your energy leak and particularly if it is a very depleting situation.

Situation:

Rating: ____

List some new ways you will **think** differently about this situation to reduce this energy drain.

List some new things you will **say** and **do** to reduce this energy drain.

List some new ways that you will **cope** with this situation to reduce this energy drain.

List the people that can help you to reduce this energy drain, and briefly describe their help.

Describe some new ways that you will "let go" and release this energy leak from your mindset in order to plug this drain. For example, after taking several deeper breaths, allow yourself to release all resistance each time you exhale by reminding yourself, "I AM letting go of ____."

CHAPTER 17
Practices Promoting Deeper Connection – Part I

The following worksheets have the purpose of encouraging spiritual practices by enabling you to schedule time each day for this to occur. This is important because even the best of intentions can get overlooked. Therefore, knowing what you will do as well as when, where, and for how long are all important steps in the process of forming and then doing the new and uplifting spiritual habits which you have decided upon.

1. Inspirational reading, which is suggested as a daily practice to learn more about your Source in addition to discovering new ways to strengthen your spiritual self, can involve an array of inspirational material including a brief passage or short reading to begin your day, longer reading periods involving traditional texts like the Bible, Quran, Torah, Bhagavad Gita, etc., and exploring a variety of spiritually-inspired books of your choice.

2. Begin by making a list of several spiritually-oriented books that you would like to read now and in the future as a part of this daily activity and discipline. One way to start this list is by asking more experienced seekers who are already on this path to provide you with some inspiring titles.

My 1st reading of the day will include (List the title or source):

When will you read?

Where will you read?

How long will you read?

My 2nd reading of the day will include (List the title or source):

When will you read?

Where will you read?

How long will you read?

CH 17: Practices Promoting Deeper Connection – Part II

Prayer or what I call "tuning-in" is a powerful way to connect to our Creator and something we do to help ourselves; plus, this suggested daily activity is as individual as those who pray.

Type of Prayers: Thank you or appreciation prayers are performed to show gratitude for your blessings (i.e., Thank you God I am grateful for my health, family, job…).

How often will you do this?   How long will you do this?
Best times for this: Best locations for this:

Type of Prayers: Prayers to help oneself in all areas of life (i.e., Thank you God for helping me to be more patient and kind, motivated, talented in my work…).

How often will you do this?   How long will you do this?
Best times for this: Best locations for this:

Type of Prayers: Prayers to help others with all issues in life. (i.e., Thank you God for helping ___ overcome their problem involving ___ to the highest good of everyone involved).

How often will you do this?   How long will you do this?
Best times for this: Best locations for this:

Type of Prayers: Forgiveness or release prayers involve asking God to forgive us for our errors, helping us to forgive ourselves, and helping us to release and forgive others who have caused us pain. (i.e., Please God forgive me for ___ and help me to forgive___ for doing/saying ___).

How often will you do this?   How long will you do this?
Best times for this: Best locations for this:

Type of Prayers: Protection prayers for others and oneself include both visible and invisible obstacles and dangers (i.e., Thank you God for protecting ___ and myself from ___ and ___).

How often will you do this?   How long will you do this?
Best times for this: Best locations for this:

Type of Prayers: Praise or reflection prayers can include songs of praise, thinking about inspirational stories, scriptural passages, ideals, ideas or prayers highlighting the awesomeness and all-ness of God, and/or simply considering His love and blessings provided to all of creation.

How often will you do this?   How long will you do this?
Best times for this: Best locations for this:

CH 17: Practices Promoting Deeper Connection – Part III

This worksheet will help you reflect upon thoughts, words, and actions that need improvement.

List the specific types of thinking, beliefs, attitudes, and mindsets (i.e., negative, stressful, low, unhappy, fearful, etc.) you often allow which require your attention, improvement, and change.

List some ways that you can begin to think differently now:

List the specific types of communication and words (i.e., critical, mean, judgmental, insulting, prejudicial, etc.) you often use which require your attention, improvement, and change.

List some ways that you will begin to communicate and speak differently now:

List the specific types of behaviors and actions (i.e., selfish, angry, inconsiderate, lustful, dishonest, etc.) you often use which require your attention, improvement, and change.

List some behaviors that will help you act differently now:

* Please note that the process of improving thoughts, words, and actions is a continuous work rather than a singular event; therefore, it requires time and consistent effort dissolving all types of darkness by turning on more light through the use of spiritual practices throughout each day.

CH 17: Practices Promoting Deeper Connection – Part IV

This worksheet will help you to reflect upon thoughts, words, actions, and practices that will strengthen your spiritual self and the connection to your Source.

Random and/or Calculated Acts of Kindness – involves giving gifts of time, service, a smile, kind words, silent encouragement or prayers, listening and attention, and/or physical goods to those in need with or without their awareness.

How often will you do this?   How long will you do this?
Best times for this: Best locations for this:

Visualization – utilizes mental imagery with or without verbal affirmations and deeper breathing in an effort to set an intention and manifest your specific desires.

How often will you do this?   How long will you do this?
Best times for this: Best locations for this:

Meditation – uses deeper breathing, a protection prayer, and a silent word (i.e., peace) or phrase (i.e., Be still and know God) for the intention of producing mental stillness and inner silence often with the purpose of listening to and connecting with the God Presence within.

How often will you do this?   How long will you do this?
Best times for this: Best locations for this:

Other practices and disciplines of your choice include:

How often will you do this?   How long will you do this?
Best times for this: Best locations for this:

List the people that will promote your spiritual growth and briefly describe their assistance.

CH 17: Practices Promoting Deeper Connection
Part V (Short Version)

Inspirational Reading.
My reading will include (list the title(s) or source(s):
How often will you do this?   How long will you do this?
Best times for this: Best locations for this:

Prayer or "Tuning-in."
Types of prayer: Thank You/Appreciation, For Self/Others, Releasing/Forgiveness, Protection, Praise/Reflection
How often will you do this?   How long will you do this?
Best times for this: Best locations for this:

Reflections on Spiritual Ideals, Ideas or Improving Thoughts, Words, and Actions.
How often will you do this?   How long will you do this?
Best times for this: Best locations for this:

<u>Thinking and thoughts</u> that need improvement:
Some ways I will think differently:

<u>Speech and words</u> that need improvement:
Some ways I will speak differently:

<u>Behaviors and actions</u> that need improvement:
Some things I will do differently:

Random and/or Calculated Acts of Kindness.
Brief description of this practice:
How often will you do this?   How long will you do this?
Best times for this: Best locations for this:

Visualization or Meditation.
Brief description of this practice:
How often will you do this?   How long will you do this?
Best times for this: Best locations for this:

Other Practices and Disciplines of Your Choice.
Brief description of this practice:
How often will you do this?   How long will you do this?
Best times for this: Best locations for this:

List the people that will help your spiritual growth and briefly describe their assistance.

CH 17: Practices Promoting Deeper Connection
Action List – Part VI (Version A)

Write the abbreviations, such as (PT), along with the time (i.e., 8:30 am) in the boxes below to indicate the specific spiritual activities that you have performed each day.

Inspirational Reading (IR) **Acts of Kindness (AK)** **Reflection Time (RT)**

Prayer Time (PT) **Meditation (M)** **Visualization (V)** **Other Practices (OP)**

MONDAY __/__/__	TUESDAY __/__/__	WEDNESDAY __/__/__	THURSDAY __/__/__	FRIDAY __/__/__	SATURDAY __/__/__	SUNDAY __/__/__

CH 17: Practices Promoting Deeper Connection
Action Checklist – Part VI (Version B)

Use as many check marks (X) in the boxes below that you need to indicate the specific amount and type of spiritual activities that you performed each day and the time this occurred. This will show you where strengths as well as weaknesses exist in your daily spiritual practices.

	Inspirational Reading (IR)	Acts of Kindness (AK)	Reflection Time (RT)	Prayer Time (PT)	Meditation or Visualization (M) or (V)	Other Practices (OP)
MONDAY __/__/__ TIME:						
TUESDAY __/__/__ TIME:						
WEDNESDAY __/__/__ TIME:						
THURSDAY __/__/__ TIME:						
FRIDAY __/__/__ TIME:						
SATURDAY __/__/__ TIME:						
SUNDAY __/__/__ TIME:						

CHAPTER 18

How to Build Spiritual Connection and Muscle Thank you Prayers

List some points under each category that you feel appreciative for in your life. Doing this enables your prayers to flow easily because you have considered what you are grateful for. Appreciation can involve anything including health, shelter, transportation, work, family, and friends. Having an attitude of gratitude keeps your energy high and opens you to greater flow.

Self/Personal Life Issues (List the things that you are thankful for: I am grateful for…)

Family/Extended Family/Relatives (Briefly note your appreciation for how these people enrich your life.)

Children/Nieces/Nephews/Unofficially Adopted Children/Pets (Briefly note your appreciation for how these people and/or animals enrich your life.)

Partner/Special Friends (Briefly note your gratitude for how these people support and enrich your life.)

Other things you are appreciative of include:

Write a personalized thank you prayer below and include statements about anything that you may be grateful for from the distant past, present, or future. (Example: Thank you God for ___, ___, and ___, and I appreciate all your Divine assistance concerning…)

CH 18: How to Build Spiritual Connection and Muscle
Praise Prayers

Praise prayers have the purpose of worshiping, honoring, and adoring God for the many blessings and awesomeness of His work, universe, and creation. Countless prayers and passages from numerous spiritual works support this category, so personal preference is the only deciding factor when it comes to selecting and then consistently using such prayers.

Write your special praise prayer below and indicate the source and its page number(s) too.

Music, song, and dance often accompany prayers that give glory to God, and this is another important way to give honor and devotion to the Almighty. Since the power of prayer is believed to increase through songs of praise, we should take every opportunity to hum, sing, play, listen, and/or dance to praise-oriented music whenever possible. With its uplifting lyrics and higher energy, praise prayers that include music certainly lie at the top of the prayer scale and should be used frequently.

List your favorite praise songs below.

Now, write any additional praise prayers that you may discover, compose, and decide to add to your toolbox of prayers. Be sure to include the source and page numbers for any special prayer.

CH 18: How to Build Spiritual Connection and Muscle Prayers for Self

List some points under each category that you wish to pray for in your life. Doing this enables such prayers to manifest more readily because you have spent time identifying your desires. Consistent prayers combined with visualization, belief, and gratitude are keys to co-creating your desires together with God.

Higher personal desires can include prayers for improved health and healing in body, mind, spirit, and Divine gifts such as greater acceptance, forgiveness, compassion, kindness, patience, and humility. List some things that you desire which can include special gifts of the Holy Spirit.

Issues involving a job, career, and vocation can include praying for...

Issues involving living arrangements, transportation, and provisions can include praying for...

Improving relationships with a partner, family members, or friends can include praying for...

Life changes involving loss from a death, moving, separation or divorce, changes in relationships, health, or ___ can include praying for...

Other things you are in need of can include praying for...

Write your personal prayer below and include statements about receiving help that you can use now and in the future. (Example: Thank you God I AM being connected to ___, and I appreciate all Divine assistance concerning...)

CH 18: How to Build Spiritual Connection and Muscle Forgiveness Prayers – Part I

Forgiveness prayers include the things we need to be forgiven for (i.e., things that we have done or failed to do that hurt others), forgiving ourselves for pain or errors we have caused, and forgiving others for the pain they caused us. **Complete the self-evaluation below for those areas in which you are in need of forgiveness.**

I have made the following mistakes concerning ___, and I will correct them by...

I have made mistakes in my thinking concerning ___, and I will correct them by...

I have made mistakes in my speech concerning ___, and I will correct them by...

I have made mistakes in my actions concerning ___, and I will correct them by...

I have made mistakes by what I have failed to do concerning ___, and I will correct them by...

I need to forgive myself for mistakes concerning ___, and I will correct them by...

Self-Evaluation for people and situations in which I need to forgive, release, and "let go."

These people ___ and events involving ___ have hurt me, so I will release/forgive them by...

CH 18: How to Build Spiritual Connection and Muscle Forgiveness Prayers – Part II

Write your forgiveness prayer below and include anything that you might need help forgiving.

CH 18: How to Build Spiritual Connection and Muscle
Prayers for Others

Prayers for others can include both general and specific needs, so consider what spiritual gifts will help most in the lives of those you will pray for. Prayers for healing, strength, general blessings, awakening, protection, prosperity, and the all-ness of God, which dissolves all forms of bondage, are good places to begin. Ending all prayers with statements such as, "Thank you for blessing this person and everyone involved to their highest good" or "Thy will be done," is an intelligent practice that enables your prayer requests to align with the receivers' divine plan and the highest good for their lives.

Prayers for parents, parental figures, mentors, siblings, and other family members can include:

Prayers for a partner, ex-partners, extended family, and special friends can include:

Prayers for children, those you teach, coach, and mentor, and special loved ones can include:

Prayers for relatives, friends, colleagues, co-workers, and teammates can include:

Prayers for the difficult people in your life, which may include greater spiritual awakening, peaceful interactions, and opening their heart to more understanding, can also include:

Prayers for those who have passed on, which may include forgiveness and experiencing peace during their transition and afterlife, can also include:

Write your prayer below and include any statements that may be helpful for others in the future.

CH 18: How to Build Spiritual Connection and Muscle Protection Prayers

Protection prayers summon safety, security, and protection for yourself and others in numerous areas of life. Consistently using such prayers can enable protection from illness and disease, accidents and injuries, various types of disasters and harm, including limiting world beliefs and actions, lower parts of our self and others, and an array of negative spiritual influences.

Prayers for personal Divine protection can also include the following points:

Prayers for Divine protection involving work, home, travel, and _____ can also include the following points:

Prayers for Divine protection involving other situations, events, and _____ can also include the following points:

Prayers for Divine protection for those in my family, including parents, siblings, my partner, and children can also include the following points:

Prayers for Divine protection for those who are extended family members, relatives, close friends, and those in most need such as _____ can also include the following points:

Write a protection prayer below that will enable Divine protection to assist yourself and everyone you include. (Example: Thank you God I AM being blessed with Divine safety, security, and protection in all ways including … (add your specific points here and other people too) – to my highest good and the good of everyone involved.)

CH 18: How to Build Spiritual Connection and Muscle Reflection/Affirmation Prayers

Reflection Prayers involve passages, phrases, or sentences found in spiritual texts (i.e., Tao Te Ching, Bible, Quran, Torah, Bhagavad Gita, etc.) that are pondered within the mind each day. By remembering and reflecting upon a spiritual idea or passage throughout the day, this keeps you spiritually connected while enabling the deeper meaning of the words to be revealed.

Write your special reflection passages below and indicate the source and its page number(s).

Affirmation prayers or God-power statements are often highly personalized and can be used to manifest specific desires in a silent, spoken, or written format. While affirmations can be found in various books, some people choose to create their own with words that fit specific prayer requests. Whenever I create affirmations, I like to use the following format: Thank you God, I AM being blessed with … (state your prayer request here) …to my highest good and the good of everyone involved in God's name. Then, I repeat my affirmation at least several times to anchor and solidify it. Thanking God in the present tense puts a blessing into process while speaking from an "I AM" presence acknowledges our inner divinity and link with our Source. The ending essentially turns the prayer results over to the Divine to create the highest good for the benefit of all.

Practice writing some of your personalized affirmation prayers using the above format.

Now write any additional affirmation prayers below that you intend to use.

CH 18: How to Build Spiritual Connection and Muscle Sustained/Guidance Prayers

Sustained prayers are longer, more powerful prayers like the Rosary and Violet Fire decrees that summon a tremendous release of Divine light. They are among the most effective ways to cleanse both ourselves and the world of error, deeper pain, and negativity of all kinds.

Write the titles of the sustained prayers below which you prefer to use and indicate the source and its page number(s) to easily access this information.

Guidance or solution prayers are used whenever you do not know what to do or how to handle a challenging situation; therefore, asking for Divine assistance makes a lot of sense during times of uncertainty. This can involve thinking and speaking God-power statements such as, "Thank you God for the positive outcome concerning these issues involving ___" or "Thank you God I AM being guided to the perfect solutions that resolve these issues completely to the highest good of everyone involved" while picturing the problem in your hands that you are now turning over to God to take care of for you.

Write your guidance or solution prayers below while including the specific situations that they involve.

CH 18: How to Build Spiritual Connection and Muscle
Creating a Prayer Chain

Creating a prayer chain is a powerful way to keep a loved one with a serious problem engulfed in Divine healing light for an extended period of time. People joining a prayer chain volunteer their time and prayers by writing their first name in a specific time slot and specifying the amount of time (i.e., 15-60 minutes) they will pray for the intended person each day over the course of a week or longer. Prayer chains, like online prayer sites, release tremendous Divine Presence and have been known to resolve difficult issues when everything else has failed.

Prayer Chain for the Week of _____ from _____ / _____ / _____ to _____ / _____ / _____

12 – 1 am
1 – 2 am
2 – 3 am
3 – 4 am
4 – 5 am
5 – 6 am
6 – 7 am
7 – 8 am
8 – 9 am
9 – 10 am
10 – 11 am
11 – 12 pm

12 – 1 pm
1 – 2 pm
2 – 3 pm
3 – 4 pm
4 – 5 pm
5 – 6 pm
6 – 7 pm
7 – 8 pm
8 – 9 pm
9 – 10 pm
10 – 11 pm
11 – 12 am

CH 18: How to Build Spiritual Connection and Muscle
Summary of All Prayers – Part I

1. Write your thank you prayer:

2. Write your praise prayer:

3. Write a prayer for yourself and your personal needs:

4. Write your forgiveness prayer:

5. Write your prayer for others:

6. Write your protection prayer:

CH 18: How to Build Spiritual Connection and Muscle
Summary of All Prayers – Part II

7. Write your reflection prayer and/or spiritual passage:

8. Write your affirmation prayer or God-power statement:

9. Write your sustained prayer:

10. Write your guidance or solution prayer:

11. Write any additional prayer(s) you discover or prefer to use:

CHAPTER 19

Unleashing Power Through Meditation
Preparation for Spiritually-Based Meditation – Part I

Answering the questions below (Y = Yes / N = No) will help you evaluate your spiritual life in order to make improvements which will better prepare you for deeper meditation practices.

Prerequisites for Meditation: Improving Your Prayer Life

Are you keeping regular times to connect and "tune-in" to the Divine with prayer? (Y / N) If not, please explain how you plan to become more consistent with these practices in the future.

If you have a current prayer practice, is this occurring during specific times? (Y / N) If yes…

When does this occur in the morning?

Where does this practice usually occur?

How long does it normally last?

When does this occur in the afternoon?

Where does this practice usually occur?

How long does it normally last?

When does this occur in the evening?

Where does this practice usually occur?

How long does it normally last?

Are you using shorter prayers to connect with the Divine throughout your day? (Y / N)

How frequently does this occur each day?

Are you using different types of prayers to stay connected throughout each day? (Y / N)

* If your prayer life is in need of some work that includes more discipline, one way to begin changing this is by setting aside certain times each day for prayer practices; this can always be combined with activities such as driving in a car, doing chores, exercising, or preparing a meal.

CH 19: Unleashing Power Through Meditation
Preparation for Spiritually-Based Meditation – Part II

Answering the questions below (Y = Yes / N = No) will help you evaluate your spiritual life in order to make improvements which will better prepare you for meditation practices.

Prerequisites for Meditation: Peeling-off Layers That Keep Us From Being Our Best

Are you becoming more aware of your thoughts and especially when negative thinking emerges and begins to take control of your mind? (Y / N) If so, (meaning yes), what do you do when this happens, and if no, what do you plan to do about reversing this trend?

Are you aware when your thoughts toward others are unkind? (Y / N) If so, how do you know?

Do you ever try to correct this? (Y / N) If so, how do you do it? If not, what is preventing you?

Are you regularly working at forgiving others and "letting go" of past pain and hurt? (Y / N) If you are, how do you do this? If not, what is preventing you from engaging in this work?

Are you aware when you are speaking unkindly to or about others? (Y / N) If so, how do you know?

Do you ever try to correct this? (Y / N) If so, how do you do this? If not, what is preventing you from engaging in this work?

* In addition to prayer practices, strengthening our connection to the Divine also involves becoming more aware of our thoughts, words, and actions since these are important steps on the path to greater self and spiritual development.

CH 19: Unleashing Power Through Meditation
Preparation for Spiritually-Based Meditation – Part III

Answering the questions below (Y = Yes / N = No) will help you evaluate your spiritual life in order to make improvements which will better prepare you for meditation practices.

Prerequisites for Meditation: Peeling-off Layers That Keep Us From Being Our Best

Do you try to avoid practices that involve criticizing, gossiping, condemning, and judging others (Y / N) and yourself? (Y / N) Discuss the times when you are most likely to struggle with these issues.

Are you aware when you are treating someone unkindly? (Y / N) How are you alerted to this?

Are you aware when your actions bring pain and harm to others (Y / N) or yourself? (Y / N)

Do you ever try to correct this? (Y / N) If so, how do you do this? If not, what is preventing you from engaging in this work?

Notice the people in your life who present the most difficulties and challenges. Are you able to make a commitment to try to improve your thoughts, words, and actions toward them? (Y / N) If so, how do you plan to do this? If not, what is preventing you from engaging in this work?

Are you regularly spending time doing practices that assist your spiritual growth? (Y / N) If so, what is working best for you? If not, what is preventing you from engaging more in this work?

* Remember that we are living our true spiritual nature only as our thoughts, words, and actions reflect our Creator each day. The good news is that engaging in divinely-focused activities releases greater light that will overcome darkness of all kinds residing within the body, mind, and spirit while also preparing us for powerful light-activating exercises such as meditation.

CH 19: Unleashing Power Through Meditation
A Guide for Practicing Spiritually-Based Meditation – Part I

Quick Steps to a Spiritually-Based Meditation

1. Choose the cleansing exercise and/or releasing prayer you will use prior to meditation.
2. Determine how you will know the meditation is finished.
3. Decide on the meditation position you will use.
4. Choose the type of breathing to use during meditation.
5. Determine the protection visualization and/or prayer you plan to use prior to meditation.
6. Decide whether to use the "Lord's Prayer" or another prayer to lead you into quietness.
7. Choose a phrase, passage, or word to return to when the mind begins to wander during the stillness.
8. Examine the method you will use to erase your mind of all thoughts as you enter into deeper silence and remain there until stronger thoughts emerge and prompt you to return to your phrase, passage, or word which begins the process again.
9. After the meditation ends, decide who or what situations will receive your prayers, positive intentions, and the greater Divine light you are releasing.
10. Decide if you will document your meditation experiences, thoughts, or feelings in a journal.
11. Be patient with yourself and the meditation process which requires consistent practice like anything else.

Gathering Important Tools for a Spiritually-Based Meditation

1. Choose the cleansing exercise and/or releasing prayer you will use prior to meditation and write these below. In the same way that working in a nuclear power plant requires special training and attire, connecting to greater Divine power always requires some type of purifying.

2. Determine how you will know the meditation is finished. Do you plan to set an alarm on a phone or clock that will let you know when your meditation is over? (Y / N) If not, briefly describe your method below.

CH 19: Unleashing Power Through Meditation
A Guide for Practicing Spiritually-Based Meditation – Part II

3. Decide on the meditation position you will use (i.e., sitting in a chair, lotus style, lying down, etc.). Also, consider and then note where you will meditate, when you will meditate, and how long this will last.

4. Choose the type of breathing you plan to use during meditation. Do you plan to use a more structured technique such as the 3-second deep breathing method, which involves a 3-second inhale, pause, 3-second exhale, and pause repeated again and again? (Y / N), or less formal breathing that perhaps includes an awareness of deeply inhaling Divine Presence and exhaling all that impedes this throughout your meditation? (Y / N) Describe your method below.

5. Determine the protection visualization and/or prayer you plan to use prior to your meditation. Do you plan to use a visualization of seeing yourself engulfed in a protective bubble of spiritual light along with other spiritual masters during your protection prayer? (Y / N) Who is the spiritual master or masters that you will summon for this? Describe your method below and write the protection prayer you plan to use for your meditation.

CH 19: Unleashing Power Through Meditation
A Guide for Practicing Spiritually-Based Meditation – Part III

6. Decide whether to use the "Lord's Prayer" or another prayer to lead you into the meditation and write this prayer below.

7. Choose a phrase (i.e., Peace in, stress out), passage, (i.e., Be still and know God) or word (i.e., Healing) to return to when the mind begins to wander during the meditation and write this below.

When using a passage such as, "Be still and know God," inhale deeply while thinking the words, "Be still," and pause for a moment before exhaling the thoughts, "Know God." When using a single word, inhale deeply while thinking a word such as, "Healing," then pause for just a moment before exhaling anything blocking and preventing healing. Pause again for a moment before repeating the process again and again for a couple of minutes at most.

8. At this point, I like to use a very brief visualization to begin the process of stilling the mind by perhaps picturing calm and still water on the surface of a pond or imagining a writing board being erased. Briefly describe the visualization you will use to accomplish this below.

As you imagine stilling your mind and allowing yourself to go further into the silence, continue to focus on your deeper breathing until stronger thoughts start to emerge. When thoughts begin to enter the mind, allow them to pass on by. Then, simply return to your phrase, passage, or word. Always refocus by silently pondering your word or phrase just briefly before returning immediately to the silence and stillness again by erasing all thoughts in your mind.

While in the silence, some people like to use sounds such as "ahh" or "ohm" that coincide with your inhalation and exhalation. This can be accomplished by inhaling deeply and pausing for a moment before exhaling with one of these sounds silently or even audibly. Then, pause for a moment before repeating the process again and again. At times, I will use the creative sound of "ahh" which represents God's name in my morning or afternoon meditations and the sound of "ohm" representing gratitude during evening meditations.

You can do away with using any words or sounds by just inhaling the image of a cleansing wave of Divine Presence overtaking you on a beach and exhaling any barriers to this as the wave returns to the ocean with all of your stress and negativity. Focusing on a wave of Divine Presence coming in with each breath you take in and the wave cleansing you as you exhale is very powerful imagery that helps to move its users into greater stillness with the Divine.

CH 19: Unleashing Power Through Meditation
A Guide for Practicing Spiritually-Based Meditation – Part IV

9. After the meditation ends, decide and then list the people and situations that will receive the prayers, positive intentions, and the greater Divine light you are releasing.

Write any prayer and/or visualization (i.e., seeing a person or difficult situation engulfed in Divine light) you plan to use following your meditation to send healing and/or blessings to help others or any special intentions.

CH 19: Unleashing Power Through Meditation
A Guide for Practicing Spiritually-Based Meditation – Part V

10. Decide if you will document your meditation experiences, thoughts, and/or feelings. Remember that this information is for your own personal use, so it can be noted in daily, weekly, or monthly entries or when you have experienced something special. Below is one way to format your written journal entries.

Day _____ Time of Day _____ (am / pm) Date ____ / ____ / ____

Location of Meditation _____

Day _____ Time of Day _____ (am / pm) Date ____ / ____ / ____

Location of Meditation _____

Day _____ Time of Day _____ (am / pm) Date ____ / ____ / ____

Location of Meditation _____

11. Always be patient with yourself and the meditation process which requires consistent practice like anything else.

CH 19: Unleashing Power Through Meditation
A Guide for Practicing Non-Spiritual Meditation – Part I

Quick Steps to a Non-Spiritual Meditation.

1. Determine how you will know the meditation is finished.
2. Decide on the meditation position you will use.
3. Choose the type of breathing you will use during the meditation before visualizing yourself in a protective bubble of white light.
4. Choose a phrase, word, or sound to continuously focus on throughout the meditation which will also coincide with each breath you take in and exhale.
5. After the meditation ends, decide who or what situations will receive your positive intentions and higher energy.
6. Decide if you will document your meditation experiences, thoughts, or feelings in a journal.
7. Be patient with yourself and the meditation process which requires consistent practice like anything else.

Gathering Important Tools for a Non-Spiritual Meditation

1. Determine how you will know the meditation is finished. Do you plan to set an alarm on a phone or clock that will let you know when your meditation is over? (Y / N) If not, briefly describe your method below.

2. Decide on the meditation position you will use (i.e., sitting in a chair, lotus style, lying down, etc.) and briefly describe this. Also, consider and then note where you will meditate, when you will meditate, and how long this will last.

CH 19: Unleashing Power Through Meditation
A Guide for Practicing Non-Spiritual Meditation – Part II

3. Choose the type of breathing you plan to use during the meditation before imagining yourself sitting in a protective bubble of white light. Do you plan to use a more structured breathing method such as the 3-second breathing method, which involves a 3-second inhale, pause, 3-second exhale, and pause repeated again and again throughout your meditation? (Y / N) or a less formal breathing technique? (Y / N) Describe your method below.

4. Choose a phrase, word, or sound to continuously focus on throughout the meditation. A word such as, "peace," "healing," "love," or any special word is fine. Some people like to focus on a specific sound such as "ahh" or "ohm." You may also choose to use a phrase such as, "I am at peace" so write your word, phrase, or sound below.

Next, simply inhale deeply while thinking a word like, "peace," then pause for just a moment before exhaling all negativity, stress, anger, sadness, fear, or any other emotion preventing peace. Then pause for a moment before repeating the process again and again.

When using a phrase such as, "I am at peace," inhale deeply while thinking the words, "I am," and pause for a moment before exhaling with the words "at peace." Then pause for a moment before repeating the process again and again.

When using a sound such as "ahh" or "ohm," inhale deeply and then pause for a moment before exhaling the sound silently or even audibly. Then pause for a moment before repeating the process again and again.

You can do away with using any words or sounds by just inhaling the image of a healing, cleansing wave overtaking you as you imagine sitting on a beach and exhaling any stress as the wave returns to the ocean with all of your negativity. Focus on a wave coming in with each breath you take in and the wave going out each time you exhale.

CH 19: Unleashing Power Through Meditation
A Guide for Practicing Non-Spiritual Meditation – Part III

5. After the meditation ends, decide who or what situations will receive your positive intentions and higher energy. Write the people's names you plan to send positive energy and/or healing to help following your meditation as well as any special intentions, situations, or events.

Describe any visualization, such as imagining a person or difficult situation engulfed in higher energy such as a cocoon of white light, which you will send to help others following your meditation.

CH 19: Unleashing Power Through Meditation
A Guide for Practicing Non-Spiritual Meditation – Part IV

6. Decide if you will document your meditation experiences, thoughts, and/or feelings. Remember that this information is for your own personal use, so it can be noted in daily, weekly, or monthly entries or when you have experienced something special. Below is one way to format your written journal entries.

Day _____ Time of Day _____ (am / pm)   Date ____/____/____

Location of Meditation _____

Day _____ Time of Day _____ (am / pm)   Date ____/____/____

Location of Meditation _____

Day _____ Time of Day _____ (am / pm)   Date ____/____/____

Location of Meditation _____

7. Be patient with yourself and the meditation process which requires consistent practice like anything else.

CHAPTER 20
Improving the "Doing" Self as a Role Model – Performance

Briefly describe a specific aspect of something you do that you would like to improve. This can relate to improving a skill, task, talent, or work-related duty that you currently perform.

List three things you will do each day that will help to improve this area of the self.

List three positive thoughts you will ponder each day that will help to improve this area of the self.

List three ways to spiritually connect/tune-in each day that will help to improve this area of the self.

List three people that will help to improve this area of the self and briefly describe their help.

List three people who will be positively influenced as you become a better role model through your improved personal performance and briefly discuss how they will be affected.

CH 20: Improving the "Doing" Self as a Role Model – Teaching

Briefly describe something you teach that you would like to improve. This can relate to improving a skill, task, or duty that you currently teach formally or informally.

List three things you will do each day that will help to improve your teaching.

List three positive thoughts you will ponder each day that will help to improve your teaching.

List three ways to spiritually connect/tune-in each day that will help to improve your teaching.

List three people that will help to improve your teaching and briefly describe their help.

List three people who will be positively influenced as you become a better teaching role model and briefly discuss how they will be affected.

CH 20: Improving the "Doing" Self as a Role Model – Mentoring

Briefly describe a specific aspect of your work as a mentor that you would like to improve. This can relate to improving a skill, task, or duty that you currently use formally or informally as a mentor. Remember that mentors differ from a role models and teachers because of the strong personal relationships they build with those they work with and impact.

List three things you will do each day that will help to improve your mentoring.

List three positive thoughts you will ponder each day that will help to improve your mentoring.

List three ways to spiritually connect/tune-in each day that will help to improve your mentoring.

List three people that will help to improve your mentoring and briefly describe their help.

List three people who will be positively influenced as you become a better mentor and briefly discuss how they will be affected.

CH 20: Improving the "Being" Self as a Role Model Overcoming Weaker Traits

Briefly describe a weaker aspect of your character that you would like to improve. This can include improving negative characteristics such as unkindness, holding grudges, gossiping, lying, anger, stealing, arrogance, enabling addictive behaviors, aggression and/or discrimination.

List three things you will do each day that will help to improve this weakness.

List three positive thoughts you will ponder each day that will help to improve this weakness.

List three ways to spiritually connect/tune-in each day that will help to improve this weakness.

List three people that will help to improve this weakness and briefly describe their help.

List three people who will be positively influenced as this weakness dissolves and briefly discuss how they will be affected.

CH 20: Improving the "Being" Self as a Role Model
Strengthening Positive Traits

Briefly describe a specific aspect of your positive characteristics that you would like to improve. This can include improving traits such as honesty, reliability, kindness, forgiveness, acceptance, patience, humility, tolerance, peace-making, generosity, and compassion.

List three things you will do each day that will help to improve this area of the self even more.

List three positive thoughts you will ponder daily that will help to improve this aspect even more.

List three ways to spiritually connect/tune-in daily that will help improve this aspect even more.

List three people that will help to improve this area of the self and briefly describe their help.

List three people who will be positively influenced as this area of the self becomes stronger and briefly discuss how they will be affected.

CH 20: Final Thoughts and Reflections for Role Models, Teachers and Mentors – Part I

Congratulations on using this challenging workbook filled with extensive inner tasks which perhaps provided some stressful moments along with many intangible gifts. Please take some time now to reflect upon and then discuss the specific kinds of learning and information that you have gained from completing the exercises and activities within this workbook.

Think about what exercises were the most difficult and the least desirable for you to do; then, discuss some of the underlying reasons that you believe may be responsible for this resistance.

CH 20: Final Thoughts and Reflections for Role Models, Teachers and Mentors – Part II

Think about what types of exercises impacted you the most and discuss your reasoning for this. Then discuss how this new learning will impact your life and the lives of others from now on.

Remember that we become stronger role models, teachers, and mentors only to the extent that we continually examine both strengths and weaknesses to improve our character and enable us to better assist those traveling along the same path. May your road to excellence be paved in peace with the wind always at your back gently guiding you to being and doing your very best.

Further Reading

Alar, C. (2021). *Understanding divine mercy: Explaining the faith series.* Stockbridge, MA: Marian Press.
Anderson, J. W. (1992). *Where angels walk.* New York: Ballantine.
Aron, E., & Aron. A. (1986). *The Maharishi effect: A revolution through meditation.* Walpole, NH: Stillpoint Publishing.

Benson, H. (1975). *The Relaxation Response.* New York: Morrow.
Borysenko, J., & Borysenko, M. (1994). *The power of the mind to heal: Renewing body, mind, and spirit.* Carson, CA: Hay House.
Brennan, B. A. (1987). *Hands of light: A guide to healing through the human energy field.* New York: Bantam Books.
Bristol, C. M. (1948). *The magic of believing: The science of setting your goal…and then reaching it.* New York: Prentice-Hall.
Bryne, R. (2006). *The secret.* New York: Simon & Schuster.
Burpo, T., & Vincent, L. (2010). *Heaven is for real: A little boy's astounding story of his trip to heaven and back.* Nashville, TN: Thomas Nelson.
Byers, A. L. (1999). *200 genuine instances of divine healing: The doctrine explained.* Anderson, IN: Gospel Trumpet Company.

Carlson, R., & Shield, B. (Eds.), (1989). *Healers on healing.* New York: Tarcher/Putnam.
Cerney, J. V. (1999). *Acupuncture without needles.* New York: Prentice Hall Press.
Chapman, G. D. (2015). *The 5 love languages: The secret to love that lasts.* Chicago: Moody Publishers (www.5lovelanguages.com).
Craig, G. (2011). *The EFT manual* (2nd ed.). Fulton, CA: Energy Psychology Press (www.emofree.com).

Diamond, J. (1979). *Your body doesn't lie: Unlock the power of your natural energy.* New York: Warner Books.
Dispenza, J. (2014). *You are the placebo: Making your mind matter.* Carlsbad, CA: Hay House.
Doherty, W. J. (2001). *Take back your marriage: Sticking together in a world that pulls us apart.* New York: Guilford Press.
Dossey, L. (1993). *Healing words: The power of prayer and the practice of medicine.* New York: HarperCollins.
Dossey, L. (1996). *Prayer is good medicine: How to reap the healing benefits of prayer.* New York: HarperCollins.
Dyer, W. W. (1997). *Manifest your destiny: The nine principles for getting everything you want.* New York: HarperCollins Publishers.
Dyer, W. W. (1998). *The secrets to manifesting your destiny.* Niles, IL: Nightingale-Conant Inc.
Dyer, W. W. (2001). *There's a spiritual solution to every problem.* New York: HarperCollins.
Dyer, W. W. (2004). *The power of intention: Learning to co-create your world your way.* Carlsbad, CA: Hay House.

Emmerich, A. C. (2004). *The life of Jesus Christ and biblical revelations: From the visions of Blessed Anne Catherine Emmerich.* (Vols. 1-4). Charlotte, NC: Tan Books.
Emoto, M. (2004). *The hidden messages in water.* Hillsboro, OR: Beyond Words Publishing.
Emoto, M. (2005). *The true power of water: Healing and discovering ourselves.* Hillsboro, OR: Beyond Words Publishing.
Epstein, G. (1989). *Healing visualizations: Creating health through imagery.* New York Bantam Doubleday Dell Publishing Group.

Feinstein, D. (2012). Acupoint stimulation in treating psychological disorders: Evidence of efficacy. *Review of General Psychology*, 16, 364-380.

Fox, E. (1931). *The golden key* (pamphlet No. 1). Marina del Rey, CA: DeVorss Publications.

Gladwell, M. (2005). *Blink: The power of thinking without thinking.* New York: Little, Brown, and Company.

Goldsmith, J. S. (1959). *The art of spiritual healing.* New York: Harper & Row.

Goldsmith, J. S. (1990). *Conscious union with God.* New York: Citadel Press.

Goldsmith, J. S. (1994). *Invisible supply: Finding the gifts of the spirit within.* New York: HarperSanFrancisco.

Gottman, J. M., & Silver, N. (1995). *Why marriages succeed or fail...and how you can make yours last.* New York: Simon & Schuster.

Gottman, J. M., & Silver, N. (1999). *The seven principles for making marriage work.* New York: Crown Publishers, Inc.

Govinda, K. (2004). *A handbook of chakra healing: Spiritual practice for health, harmony, and inner peace.* Old Saybrook, CT: Konecky & Konecky.

Green, J. (2012). *The reiki healing bible: Transmit healing energy through your hands to achieve deep relaxation, inner peace, and total well-being.* London: Quantum Publishing Ltd.

Greenberg, J. S. (2011). *Comprehensive stress management* (12th ed.). New York: McGraw-Hill.

Hawkins, D. R. (2007). *Power vs. force, the hidden determinants of human behavior: An anatomy of consciousness.* West Sedona, AZ: Veritas Publishing.

Hay, L. L. (1984). *You can heal your life.* Carlsbad, CA: Hay House.

Hirshberg, C., & Barasch, M, I. (1995). *Remarkable recovery: What extraordinary healings tell us about getting well and staying well.* New York: Riverhead Books.

Hopson, J. L., Donnatelle, R. J., & Littrell. (2009). *Get fit, stay well.* New York: Pearson Education.

Hunter, C., & Hunter, F. (1981). *How to heal the sick.* Kingwood, TX: Hunter Books.

Hunter, C., & Hunter, F. (1987). *Handbook for healing: Supplement to how to heal the sick.* Kingwood, TX: Hunter Books.

Insel, P. M., & Roth, W. T. (2013). *Core concepts in health* (13th ed). New York: McGraw-Hill.

Klauser, H. A. (2000). *Write it down, make it happen.* New York: Simon & Schuster, Inc.

Lin, C. (2000). *Spring forest qigong course manual level 1.* Minnetonka, MN: Learning Strategies Corporation.

Lin, C. (2001). *Spring forest qigong for healing level 2.* Minnetonka, MN: Learning Strategies Corporation.

Lin, C. (2003). *SFQ – Level three for advanced energy development and healing.* Minneapolis, MN: Spring Forest Qigong Publishing.

Lin, C. (2011). *Head-to-toe-healing: Your body's repair manual.* Spring Forest Qigong Publishing (www.springforestqigong.com).

Lin, C., & Rebstock, G. (2003). *Born a healer: I was born a healer. You were born a healer, too!* Minneapolis, MN: Spring Forest Publishing.

MacNutt, F. (2005). *Healing: Revised and expanded – the bestselling classic.* Notre Dame, IN: Ave Maria Press.

McArthur, B. (1993). *Your life: Why it is the way it is and what you can do about it: Understanding the universal laws.* Virginia Beach, VA: ARE Press.

McGee, C. T., & Chow, E. P. Y. (1995). *Qigong: Miracle healing from China.* Coeur d'Alene, ID: MediPress.

McTaggart, L. (2002). *The field: The quest for the secret force of the universe.* New York: HarperCollins.

Moody, R. A. (1976). *Life after life.* Covington, GA: Mockingbird.

Moody, R. A. (1989). *The light beyond.* New York: Ballantine.

Murphy, J. (1965). *The amazing laws of cosmic mind power.* West Nyack, NY: Parker Publishing Company.

Myss, C. (1996). *Anatomy of the spirit: The seven stages of power and healing.* New York: Three Rivers Press.

Myss, C. (1996). *Energy anatomy: The science of personal power, spirituality, and health.* Louisville, CO: Sounds True, Inc.

Myss, C. (1997). *Why people don't heal and how they can.* New York: Three Rivers Press.

Myss, C. (1999). *The Caroline Myss audio collection.* Boulder, Co: Sounds True, Inc.

Myss, C. (2001). *Scared contracts: Awakening your divine potential.* New York: Random House.

Myss, C. (2001). *Advanced energy anatomy: The science of co-creation and your power of choice.* Louisville, CO: Sounds True, Inc.

Myss, C. (2004). *Invisible acts of power: Channeling grace in your everyday life.* New York: Free Press.

Myss, C. (2007). *Entering the castle: An inner path to God and your soul.* New York: Free Press.

Osteen, D. (2003). *Healed of cancer.* Houston, TX: Lakewood Church.

Pappas, N. T. (2022). *Discovering your excellence within: A holistic guide to being your best.* Big Rapids, MI: Millpond Books.

Pelletier, K. R. (1977) *Mind as healer mind as slayer: A holistic approach to preventing stress disorders.* New York: Dell Publishing Company.

Ponder, C. (1971). *Open your mind to prosperity.* Marina del Rey, CA: DeVorss Publications.

Ponder, C. (1984). *The dynamic laws of prosperity.* Camarillo, CA: DeVorss & Company.

Ponder, C. (1985). *The dynamic laws of healing.* Marina del Rey, CA: DeVorss & Company.

Ponder, C. (1987). *The dynamic laws of prayer.* Marina del Rey, CA: DeVorss Publications.

Prophet, E. C. (1997). *Violet flame: To heal body, mind, & soul.* Gardiner, MT: Summit University Press (www.summituniversitypress.com).

Prophet, M. L., & Prophet, E. C. (1984). *The science of the spoken word.* Livingston, MT: Summit University Press (www.summituniversitypress.com).

Randolph, L. (2005). *Spirit talk: Hearing the voice of God.* Wilkesboro, NC: MorningStar Publications.

Redfield, J. (1993). *The celestine prophecy: An adventure.* New York: Warner Books.

Ritchie, G. G., & Sherrill, E. (1993). *Return from tomorrow.* Grand Rapids, MI: Baker.

Rossman, M. L. (2000). *Guided imagery for self-healing: An essential resource of anyone seeking wellness.* Novato, CA: New World Library.

Roth, R. (1997). *Divine dialogue: How to heal your life with living prayer.* Niles, IL: Nightingale-Conant.

Roth, R., & Occhiogrosso, P. (1997). *The healing path of prayer: A modern mystic's guide to spiritual power.* New York: Three Rivers Press.

Salem, H., & Salem, C. (1997). *The presence of angels in your life.* Shippensburg, PA: Destiny Image Publishers, Inc.

Sanford, A. (1972). *The healing light.* New York: Random House.

Schneidman, S., Cave, J., Foreman, L., & Hicks, J (Eds.). (1989). *Mysteries of the unknown series: Powers of healing.* Richmond, VA: Time-Life Books, Inc.

Seaward, B, L. (2004). *Managing stress: Principles and strategies for health and well-being (4th ed.)* Sudbury, MA: Jones and Bartlett.

Silva, J., & Stone, R. B. (1989). *You the healer: The world-famous Silva method on how to heal yourself and others.* Tiburon, CA: H J Kramer Inc.

Simonton, O., C., Mathews-Simonton, S., & Creighton, J. (1992). *Getting well again: The bestselling classic about the Simonton's revolutionary lifesaving self-awareness techniques.* New York: Bantam Books.

Sinetar, M. (1986). *Ordinary people as monks and mystics: Lifestyles for self-discovery.* Mahwah, NJ: Paulist Press.

Stearn, J. (1985). *Soulmates.* New York: Bantam Books.

Steiger, B., & Hansen Steiger, S. (2004). *Miracles of healing: Inspirational stories of amazing recovery.* Avon, MA: Adams Media.

Sugrue, T. (1997). *The story of Edgar Cayce: There is a river.* Virginia Beach, VA: ARE Press.

The Association for Research and Enlightenment. *The Edgar Cayce Readings.* Virginia Beach, VA. (www.EdgarCayce.org).

The boy who saw true. (1953). Anonymous Author. Essex, England: The C.W. Daniel Company LTD.

The original pieta prayer book. (1972). Miraculous Lady of Roses (www.mlor.com). Hickory Corners, MI.

Todeschi, K. J. & Reed, H. (2014). *Contemporary Cayce: A complete exploration using today's philosophy and science.* Virginia Beach, VA: A.R.E. Press.

Tolle, E. (1999). *The power of now: A guide to spiritual enlightenment.* Novato, CA: Namaste Publishing and New World Library.

Tolle, E. (2005). *A new Earth: Awakening to your life's purpose.* New York: The Penguin Group.

Varga, J. (2013). *Divine visits.* Virginia Beach, VA: 4th Dimension Press.

Ward, T. (2001). *Meditation & dreamwork: Create a better life through the power of inner reflection and dreams.* Edison, NJ: Castle Books.

Weiss, B. L. (1993). *Through time into healing: Discovering the power of regression therapy to erase trauma and transform mind, body, and relationships.* New York: Simon & Schuster.

Yogananda, P. (1946). *Autobiography of a yogi.* New York: The Philosophical Library.

Zukav, G., & Francis, L. (2001). *The heart of the soul: Emotional awareness.* New York.

Acknowledgements

Many people played a role in helping me complete this project spanning over 18 years, and I would like to recognize and thank these people for all their time, ideas, and assistance. My appreciation goes out to Pamela Sipe, Dr. Cathy Ely-Grover, Dawn Miles, Peter Woodbury, and Elaine Wetzel for providing helpful ideas which I was able to ponder and then adapt to create useful exercises in this workbook. Additional thanks go out to Elaine Wetzel for her editing and insights which helped to enhance this entire workbook. A special thanks to all my clients and students who tested these exercises and provided important implicit and explicit information about the effectiveness of the tools and strategies they used. I am also grateful to my academic advisers Dr. Patrick McKenry, Dr. Tom Davis, Dr. Tim Curry, Dr. Jere Schultz, Dr. Steven Gavazzi, and Dr. Albert Davis for all of their guidance and support.

    I also want to acknowledge the many coaches, athletes, administrators, and friends who contributed to my development as an athlete, coach, and individual in addition to those who provided special wisdom and experiences anonymously which were used to convey important learning. My special thanks to Joe Battista, John Tortorella, Jon Shellington, Larry Rocha, Darren Hersh, Dr. Craig McCarthy, Dr. Greg Austin, Jim Gilmore, Toby O'Brien, Scott Allen, Henry Brabham, Dave Rose, Morris "Moose" Lallo, Ricky Schiermer, Lennert Sundberg, Jerry York, Bill Wilkinson, Tom Newton, Terry Flanagan, Pat "Whitey" Stapleton, Dickie Moore, Gaeten Picard, Bobby Rousseau, Gaston Drapeau, Jacques Demers, Eddie Swiss, Father David Kline, Randy Ehrsam, Pete Iussig, Sam Samardzija, Dr. Christine Price, Dr. Stephanie Griffin, Dr. Kevin Bush, Dr. Suzanne Klatt, Kerri Warner, Judie Hord, L. Jensen, Doris Nielsen, Mark DiVincenzo, Scott Jolly, John Bacon, the Tempest, Sipe, Montebell, Dexter, McQuillan, Fardelmann, Moran, Moore, David, Mowitz, Califano, Brueckman, Krutz, Devaney, Stapleton, and Rose families.

    My special appreciation extends to my excellent book designer and production specialist Laura Smyth from Smythtype Design whose patience, flexibility, and perseverance—especially during the pandemic which continually challenged and slowed progress—were as impressive as her work ethic and expertise. All of your time, insights, and dedication greatly enhanced my long-term project, so a big thanks again.

    I would also like to thank my family for all of their love and support during this project as well as during my athletic career, life-long studies, and throughout the many tasks that I have pursued over the years. Many thanks go out to my mom, my dad and his partner Elaine, my sister Val and her husband Randy, my sister Kim and her husband Jamie, my nephews Matt, Mark and his wife Rachael, and my brother Chris and his wife Melissa. Your encouragement and support in numerous ways have been both helpful and much appreciated.

    Finally and by far the most impacting person I would like to acknowledge is my special partner and wife Lori, who has been my primary editor, artist, and amazing friend, for all your love and the many ways you have assisted me over the years. Your continuing support, insights, and guidance have helped to enrich my life and all of my books in countless ways which would not have occurred without your time, effort, and vision. Thank you, thank you, thank you for being the giving, loving, and uplifting soul that you are and have been throughout the years. I love you and I am grateful to have met such a special lady to accompany me during my mission, purpose, work, and unique life path. In essence, you inspire and help to keep my light burning so very bright.

About the Author

Nick Pappas, Ph.D., LPC., NCC., brings a unique background, with an inspiring and empowering presence, to his clients and audiences with more than 35 years of experiences that highlight a rare combination of practical, athletic, and academic achievement. As a diligent, life-long seeker of wisdom, truth, and excellence, Dr. Pappas completed a doctorate degree in human development and family science with a minor in sociology of sport from The Ohio State University. Prior to this, he earned a master's degree in counselor education from The Ohio University and a bachelor's degree in kindergarten and elementary education from The Pennsylvania State University.

The creation of his book *Discovering Your Excellence Within: A Holistic Guide to Being Your Best* and this accompanying workbook involved more than 18 years of intensive study, research, and contemplative writing. This persistence resulted in an extraordinary approach for elevating performance and strengthening all aspects of the holistic self. Achievers, who recognize and value the pursuit of excellence in combination with greater self-development and self-mastery, will find these volumes filled with uplifting information and practical, life-enhancing strategies, which can help to bring out the best in who you are and all that you do. Discovering and then learning to utilize an array of innate, yet often hidden, abilities are an incredible opportunity awaiting those who are eager to excel on their path.

Residing at the opposite end of the spectrum from *Discovering Your Excellence Within*, Dr. Pappas' doctoral dissertation, *On the Ice and Off the Rink: A Qualitative Study of Hockey Players' Aggression*, exposed different types of out-of-sport athlete aggression through interviews with 23 collegiate and/or minor professional athletes. This work served as the foundation for his first book, *The Dark Side of Sports: Exposing the Sexual Culture of Collegiate and Professional Athletes*, because the information that Pappas discovered and withheld from his dissertation included sexually deviant, but not necessarily aggressive behavior. This project expanded to include interviews with 142 collegiate, minor, and major league athletes representing five prominent U.S. sports, although virtually every male collegiate sport is noted within these research findings.

As a university adjunct professor, Dr. Pappas has taught undergraduate and graduate-level classes including sociology of sport, counseling, sport marketing, health and wellness, fitness, and strength training at several state universities. His academic publications and presentations have addressed out-of-sport athlete aggression, family, and counseling-related issues. Pappas' captivating study, *Athlete Aggression on the Rink and Off the Ice: Athlete Violence and Aggression in Hockey and Interpersonal Relationships*, continues to draw significant attention from academic scholars and students alike.

Presentations based on his groundbreaking book, *The Dark Side of Sports: Exposing the Sexual Culture of Collegiate and Professional Athletes*, address the sexually deviant and aggressive behaviors occurring at a variety of levels of sports beginning in high school in an effort to prevent these negative practices while promoting greater levels of personal and team excellence in the process. Incorporating innovative ideas with supporting material from his book *Discovering Your Excellence Within* and workbook, Dr. Pappas enjoys promoting greater self-development, self-mastery, and the pursuit of excellence in addition to stress and energy management using a holistic approach to impact multiple aspects of the self through his counseling and life coaching work, presentations, and teaching.

Dr. Pappas is a Licensed Professional Counselor (LPC), a National Board Certified Counselor (NCC), and a certified hypnotherapist with over 23 years of experience that includes working as a mental health therapist, an adult and adolescent drug and alcohol counselor, a school counselor (grades 5-12), a teenage group home counselor, and as a professional holistic counselor/life coach in private practice. As a teacher at the elementary, middle, and high school level, he has taught a variety of subjects, including industrial arts, physical education, and strength training, in addition to a year of instructing high school theology classes. Most importantly, these diverse experiences have provided ample opportunities for Pappas to use his holistic approach to assist both clients and students alike in overcoming many types of stressful challenges and concerns.

As a hockey coach, Dr. Pappas worked as an assistant coach for the Johnstown Chiefs of the East Coast Hockey League (ECHL), which was the AA minor professional affiliate for the NHL's Calgary Flames. Prior to this, he coached The Ohio State University Women's Club Hockey Team during his doctoral program. While earning a master's degree at Ohio University in the areas of school, college, and mental health counseling, he served as an assistant coach for the OU men's ice hockey team, helping the Bobcats to win back-to-back league, playoff, and national championships. Dr. Pappas has been an instructor and coach for over 26 years at youth camps and sports clinics, including The Penn State Hockey Camp.

As a minor professional hockey player for five seasons, Dr. Pappas played on championship teams in his first three seasons and was his team's captain during his third championship season. He gained invaluable experience during the last two championships, which were won under the NHL's 2004 Stanley Cup winning coach John Tortorella. He played his final two seasons of professional hockey in Europe – first in Sweden and then in Denmark as a player-coach. As a collegiate athlete, Pappas played a season as a "walk-on" at Division I Bowling Green State University before transferring to Penn State University. At PSU, where he earned a bachelor's degree in elementary education, he was part of a national championship team and received the team's Most Valuable Player Award. Overall, Nick has been a part of six championship teams during his elite-level hockey career – two as a collegiate coach, three as a minor professional athlete, and one as a collegiate athlete. Dr. Pappas was inducted into the Andrean High School Sports Hall of Fame and the Penn State Hockey Hall of Fame in 2004.

Seldom do authors, teachers, and counselors have the luxury of drawing on the extraordinarily diverse career opportunities that Dr. Nick Pappas has experienced. Nick's participation in collegiate and professional sports as a player and a coach has equipped him with a unique perspective and powerful approach for elevating performance as well as all aspects of the body, mind, and spirit. These experiences, combined with practical and academic knowledge and understanding, provide exceptional resources that enable and empower Dr. Pappas' ability to teach, motivate, and inspire his diverse audiences and the clients he counsels and coaches. He resides in central Michigan with his wife Lori and can be contacted through his website (www.DrNickPappas.com).

Final Blessing

May the Hand of the Divine heal, awaken, protect, and bless everyone who touches and is touched by any aspect of this work. May the Spirit of the Almighty enable and empower this work to be tremendously impacting and influence multitudes by promoting positive change, holistic excellence, transformational decision-making, higher states of consciousness, and a release of Infinite All-ness that frees people from all types of bondage, oppression, and darkness as it uplifts all parts of the soul, body, mind, and spirit to the highest good of everyone involved.

www.ingramcontent.com/pod-product-compliance
Lightning Source LLC
Chambersburg PA
CBHW081615100526
44590CB00021B/3444